Christopher C. Andrews

Report to the Department of state

On the forests and forest-culture of Sweden

Christopher C. Andrews

Report to the Department of state
On the forests and forest-culture of Sweden

ISBN/EAN: 9783337727291

Printed in Europe, USA, Canada, Australia, Japan

Cover: Foto ©ninafisch / pixelio.de

More available books at **www.hansebooks.com**

REPORT

TO

THE DEPARTMENT OF STATE

ON THE

FORESTS AND FOREST-CULTURE OF SWEDEN.

BY

C. C. ANDREWS,

MINISTER RESIDENT OF THE UNITED STATES TO SWEDEN AND NORWAY.

REPORT

FORESTS AND FOREST-CULTURE OF SWEDEN

BY

C. C. ANDREWS,

MINISTER RESIDENT OF THE UNITED STATES TO SWEDEN AND NORWAY.

Mr. Andrews to Mr. Fish.

LEGATION OF THE UNITED STATES,
Stockholm, August 5, 1872. (Received September 25.)

SIR: I have the honor to send herewith a report which I have prepared on the forest and forest-culture of Sweden. It comprises a practical description of the manner of growing and the economical management and use of forests, as well as a translation of some of the principal laws on the administration, care, and preservation of public forests and for the support of instruction in forestry.

I also transmit four different treatises, in Swedish, on forest-culture, cited in the report; also, a report of a commission in regard to further legislation concerning the forests.

The commission first mentioned recommend legislation in Sweden similar to what obtains in many other countries of Europe, prohibiting owners of private forests from cutting, for commercial purposes, trees under a certain size. The fact that some kinds of trees require several generations for their full development, and that the climate and supply of water in a country are much influenced by the existence or non-existence of forests, affords strong grounds for such a law.

Trusting that this document may be of some help in shaping the much-needed legislation in the United States for promoting regrowth and the preservation of forests, I remain, &c.,

C. C. ANDREWS.

To the Honorable HAMILTON FISH,
Secretary of State, &c., &c., &c.

REPORT TO THE DEPARTMENT OF STATE BY C. C. ANDREWS, MINISTER RESIDENT OF THE UNITED STATES TO SWEDEN AND NORWAY, ON THE FORESTS AND FOREST CULTURE OF SWEDEN.

CONTENTS

I.—NATURE AND EXTENT OF THE FORESTS OF SWEDEN.

The great mass of the forests of Sweden is found in the north central part of the country, and consists principally of the so-called Scotch pine and the white or Norway spruce, both of which grow to great size and are highly esteemed for their timber. The common European oak has its natural northern boundary along the river Dal, but is cultivated up to Lundsvall, in latitude 62° 20'. It is a splendid tree, a favorite ornament of parks, and produces timber superior to the American white oak. The beech abounds in the south part of the kingdom, and is cultivated even north of Upsala. However, the species most numerous, next to the fir, is the white birch, which has a beautiful drooping foliage and is useful for timber. It is found in all the forests and is not unfrequently used for avenues at county seats. It furnishes the principal fuel. The lime (in Swedish, *lim*) makes a handsome and vigorous tree, and it is not uncommon to see it forming splendid avenues a couple of centuries old. The gray alder is very common and merits particular notice on account of its large size. The elm, (less stately than the American,) the soft maple, the ash, the poplar, the hawthorn, (oxel,) large and handsome, are also common.

On the whole, Sweden appears to be a natural forest country. Nor is the climate unfavorable to a fair variety and hardy growth of trees. Observations at Stockholm, from 1754 to 1863—one hundred and nine years—show that the extreme of heat during that time was 96°.8, and the extreme of cold 25°.6 below zero, Fahrenheit. At Hapacanda, the most northerly port, also in Jemtland, the mercury frequently freezes. [For some remarks on the fruit-trees of Sweden, see report on the agriculture of Sweden, "Commercial Relations United States, 1870," p. 385.]

In 1850, the then chief director of the Forest Institute estimated the area of land in Sweden which bears, or is suitable for bearing, forest at 30,000,000 acres, which agrees with the estimate of other authorities; and he expressed the opinion that if forest-growing was properly attended to the country would not only have enough product therefrom for its own use, but a quantity for export, which, at the then increased price of lumber in southern countries, would be more profitable than the export of iron. He maintained, however, that forest economy up to that time had been managed with the greatest want of care.

Mr. Forsell, in a paper on this subject, published in 1844, shows that a lack of timber was beginning to be felt in many parts of Sweden, and states that Stora, Kopparberg, and Gefleborg were the only counties so rich in forests as to be sure of their preservation for a long term of years without an improved system of forest economy. And he adds that, if such a system shall not be established, the whole country will soon suffer for the want of forests.

As, proof, however, of the efforts in this regard which were being adopted by the Forest Institute, as well as the Iron Office, it may be mentioned that on Wising's Island 700 acres were planted with oaks, the sand plains of Christianstad and Holland counties were planted with trees, and improvements were made in the royal parks.

At present one sees along the principal routes of travel a generous supply of forest, though the trees are mostly young; and the surface of the country, being agreeably undulating and abundantly supplied with clear streams and lakes, tends to produce a favorable impression. The growth of young forest on patches too rocky for tilling, or even grazing, and the scattered seed-trees left standing in places where wood or timber has been cut off in the larger forests, remind the traveler of the attention to forest-culture which is becoming general.

The annual growth or production of forest may be calculated, says Thomée, at 22 famns, (a Swedish "famn" is a little less than a cord,) of 100 cubic feet Swedish, per tunnland—say 20 cords per acre, a tunnland being equal to 1.22 acres—estimating the time of regrowth at 100 years, usual in the south and middle parts of Sweden, so that 300,000 acres growth out of the 30,000,000 acres are consumed annually, and the annual product according to the present resources of the forest is 6,000,000 cords.

The consumption of forest is calculated by Forsell at 7,230,000 famns yearly, including the export of boards and heavy timber. Ström estimates it at 7,755,200 famns; Langberg, again considering the increase of population for the present, at least 8,865,200 famns. Supposing the production to amount to 5,700,000 famns, there occurs, says Thomée, a yearly lack of 3,165,000 famns, which should be supplied in a way not to draw on the forest for more than it can yield. According to the opinion of experts, if cultivation is properly attended to, the Swedish forests can supply that need and a considerable surplus.

The export of all sorts of timber and wood from Sweden in 1870 amounted to 109,000,000 cubic feet, besides 14,000,000 sticks of wood and other timber. The total area of forest-land under the care of the administration of forests is 5,000,000 acres.

	Rix-dollars.
The receipts from the sale of timber and wood from the public forests for the year 1870 were	438,301 27
Expenses for same period	354,038 06
Leaving a balance of	84,263 21

Of the expenses there were appropriated:

For the bureau of administration	21,800
For the Forest Institute	15,300
For the forest schools	25,400

For the purpose of forest administration, the kingdom is divided into six districts, with a forest inspector, and about twelve "jäg mästare" (hunting-master or forester) for each district.

II.—HISTORICAL SKETCH OF FOREST ADMINISTRATION.

Most of the countries of Europe, and Sweden among them, appear to have borrowed the principal part of their forest science from Germany, which has long occupied the foremost position in respect to forest administration and forest literature.

Forest regulations were issued by the Swedish government as early as 1647; and even before that, private owners were required by law to plant and protect from cattle two timber trees for every one cut. The owners of privileged estates were exempted from this last requirement by the diet of 1734, but it continued to apply to tax-paying estates and to crown-lands leased to private persons till 1789. Regulations for the forest were again issued in 1793, but they were soon found unsatisfactory, and in 1798 a commission was appointed, consisting of six persons, to devise new regulations, which, after five years' labor, reported an amendment of fifteen sections of the forest regulations, and their project was finally confirmed and issued in the form of forest regulations, August 1, 1805. The same day a royal circular letttor was sent to each of the county or provincial governments, ordering a project to be presented for a law on the duty of replanting forests. Shortly afterward, Professor F. W. Radloff was commissioned to visit Germany to study its forest system, and his report was submitted, in 1809, to the before-mentioned commission. The subject was, in 1810, remitted by the diet to the administration of marine affairs and the bureau of public or crown lauds and of mines; which, after the provincial governors had expressed their opinion thereon, recommended (1819) that each county or provincial government should work out a plan adapted to its own locality, and that a committee for the whole kingdom might then be appointed to prepare a final project for a law on this subject. The matter was taken up in the cabinet in 1820, but was postponed till 1823, in order to be united with a law for the sale of crown timber; and the result was that regulations for the crown forests were issued by the government in 1824. Early in 1828, a committee of three persons was appointed by the government to report a project for the economy of public and private forests and amendments to the laws in regard to hunting. The committee reported the same year in favor of the establishment of a forest institute, to be located in the deer park, close to Stockholm, of suitable instruction in hunting, and the establishment of a central bureau or administration for the management of forest affairs. The government established the institute, and confirmed the plan for its operation. The committee, on further consideration, being of opinion that the administrative duties could be performed by the chief director of the institute, the government postponed establishing the central bureau of administration, but charged the committee to prepare a new plan of instruction in regard to hunting and the management of forests. Report having been made as to the principles which should obtain therein, the committee was again, in 1836, ordered to report regulations in conformity with such principles for instruction in the forest and hunting establishment. Their projects were presented in 1837, and the government issued an order embodying the same March 16, 1838.

Influenced by the action of the sixth Swedish national agricultural fair of 1853, no less than by that of the diet in 1853 and 1854, the government appointed a committee to report a project as to what means, either through the legislative or executive branches of the government, could further be adopted to obviate in the future the then complained of lack of forests and the injurious climatic effects arising from their destruction. Their report was handed in June 28, 1856, embracing a plan for the management of forests, and action thereon was taken in 1859, when the bureau of forest administration was created.

III.—FOREST LEGISLATION AND OFFICIAL REGULATIONS.

1. Remarks on the report of the commission of 1868.

In pursuance of a resolution of the diet of May 13, 1868, the King, on the 18th June of that year, appointed a special commission, of which Mr. E. V. Almquist, member of the first chamber, was chairman, to inquire into the need of further legislation in relation to forests and to report a bill for a law on the subject. Their report was submitted the 21st December, 1870, and, with the bill accompanying it, makes 392 printed pages, besides numerous tables. One clause in the reported bill is the compulsory feature, which, though less stringent, is in the spirit of enactments now in force in all of the countries of Europe that have given much attention to forest administration, namely, that owners of private forests shall not, under a penalty of from five to five hundred rix dollars, cut therefrom and dispose, for commercial purposes, trees that are less than 8.3 inches in diameter at a distance of 16 Swedish feet from the large end, or less than 11 inches in diameter at the large end. (See §§ 42 and 90.) A copy of the document will accompany this report. The subject is expected to be considered in the diet of 1873.

[Translation from the Swedish.]

2. *His Royal Majesty's gracious instruction for the forest administration and the forest corps, given at the palace of Stockholm, November 19, 1869.*

§ 1. The object of the forest administration, assorting under the royal department of the finances, shall be to promote a suitable forest economy and chase within the kingdom, and shall, in this regard, as far as it is their duty, according to this instruction or other regulations in force, themselves take suitable measures for this purpose or humbly propose to His Royal Majesty the taking of the same. It shall be the special duty of the administration to direct and superintend the management of the crown-parks, the quicksand fields, commons and forests of the farms belonging to the Crown, which, as separately prescribed, have been placed under the care of the forest corps, and also to see that the care and use of other common forests and quicksand fields belonging to private persons are properly superintended.

§ 2. Concerning the business of the forest administration in regard to the selection of suitable localities in the læns of Rapparberg and Norrland, as crown-parks, partly during the survey and partly of land, which not yet has been subject to a general survey, special regulations are issued and in force; and the administration shall not decide about the selection for crown-parks of unsurveyed land, or of land not being surveyed, before communities and private persons, who consider themselves owners of the land, have had opportunity to report and prove their claims; and the decision shall be submitted to the judgment of His Royal Majesty before being put into execution.

§ 3. Concerning the survey of public forests for a regulated management, the forest administration shall issue necessary rules, in accordance with such principles, as are approved of by His Royal Majesty; and the administration shall appoint ordinary or extra officers of the forest corps or schools to survey, whenever suitable, the above-mentioned forests, and not only examine the same after the survey has been completed, and approve of the plan for the management, with or without altering the same, but also to afterward prescribe necessary modifications of the management or alterations of the approved plan which, at the revision of the same, may be found suitable.

§ 4. Having examined the projects and calculations which, according to § 41, here below, shall be annually transmitted by the district directors, ("jägmästare,") the forest administration will decide about the forest cultivation and other work to be done during the coming year at the common or public parks, committed to the care of the forest corps as well as to fix the amount of the expenditures not to be exceeded. In regard to crown-parks and quicksand fields belonging to the Crown, the decision of the administration may, however, not be given to the respective officers to be carried into effect before the general project mentioned in § 10 has been approved of by His Royal Majesty.

§ 5. Concerning the business of the forest administration in regard to the felling of oak-trees and large timber-trees, which private parties have not acquired unlimited right to dispose of, otherwise than for the account of the Crown, is especially prescribed.

§ 6. In regard to the public-forest schools, it shall be the duty of the forest administration to carefully superintend that the instruction is so regulated and managed that the objects of the school are attained; and the administration shall assign forests for the practical exercises of the pupils at the Forest Institute, as well as upon the proposal of the manager of the institute distribute stipends among the pupils.

§ 7. Officers and attendants at the forest corps, as well as at the forest-schools, shall be subordinate to the forest administration, which shall issue necessary regulations for the due exercising of their functions.

§ 8. The forest administration shall also superintend the dwelling-places, farms, and localities assigned to the forest corps and schools, and shall see to that their farms and localities are not otherwise used or disposed of than according to issued regulations, and that they are respectively surveyed and examined; and a copy of the record of each such survey shall be transmitted to the forest administration.

§ 9. A complete ground-rent book shall be kept by the forest administration, in which the dwelling-places, farms and localities assigned to the forest corps and schools shall be entered, as well as the crown-parks and the quicksand fields belonging to the Crown, and also other public forests, as soon as they are subjected to a proper forest management.

§ 10. Of the funds assigned for forest purposes from the seventh title of the budget, the administration will dispose, according to the rules issued by His Royal Majesty, of that part thereof which His Royal Majesty shall determine. The forest administration will, every year, in the month of November, render to His Royal Majesty, for approval, a general project for the use during the coming year of the above-mentioned funds placed at the disposal of the administration, thereby observing to retain sufficient amount, to be assigned in case of necessity by His Royal Majesty to fill unforeseen wants which may occur during the course of the year.

§ 11. Toward the defraying of respectively-fixed expenses for crown-parks, quicksand fields belonging to the Crown, and for the forests of the dwelling-places managed by the forest corps, necessary funds ought to be advanced in the manner prescribed by the forest administration and upon the requisition of the respective district directors from the treasury of the province, to be repaid when used for forests belonging to dwelling-places, by what they yield and otherwise out of the funds assigned for forest purposes and placed at the disposal of the administration, it being the duty of the forest administration, the general project and the working-plan for the year having been approved. to inform all the administrations of the Provinces of the sales which they have to observe in regard to similar advances.

§ 12. For the paying of such advances made by the treasuries of the provinces, according to the foregoing section, which ought to be refunded from the funds for forest purposes, placed at the disposal of the forest administration, as stated in § 10, as well as for the defraying of other expenses which His Royal Majesty has decided to be paid out of the same funds, the forest administration will. on application, receive from the exchequer out of the assigned funds the requisite amount, either by draft upon the respective treasuries or, if at any time such may be convenient, in cash.

§ 13. The accounts which the district director shall render according to § 43, here below. to His Royal Majesty's governor of the provinces, and to be transmitted from here to the forest administration, shall not only all the accounts of delivered forest objects, but also the accounts of the funds received by the district director, which regard Crown-parks, quicksand fields belonging to the Crown, and forests belonging to dwelling-places, the yield of which shall go the royal treasury, be fully revised by the administration, whereas the accounts of the latter, and in regard to other forests belonging to dwelling-places or commons, the revising of which as to ciphers is done elsewhere, shall be revised by the forest administration with regard to the manner in which the received funds have been employed according to the accounts of the district director. The forest administration shall also fully revise the accounts of the public forest schools. Should, at the revision, any errors be found in the accounts, the forest administration will decide about the same, having, where such is necessary, heard the explanation of the respective parties.

§ 14. It shall be the duty of the forest administration to examine the complaints which in prescribed order are entered against the decision of, or steps taken by the forest officers in such cases, when appeal, according to regulations, may take place.

§ 15. In regard to questions concerning the forest and chase, the forest administration shall render the reports which may be required by His Royal Majesty or by the authorities. Whereas the administration shall, for the explanation of occurrent affairs, demand the opinion of His Royal Majesty's governors of the provinces, of the directors of the forest schools, and of the officers of the forest corps; also, on application, receive the assistance of H's Royal Majesty's governor of the province, whenever required for the execution of the decisions of the administration, the administration being allowed every year. when necessary, to request the attendance of the forest inspectors at the meeting of the administration, to jointly decide about the exercising of rules or measures ordered for the development of the forest management.

§ 16. Not later than the 31st of December every year the forest administration shall transmit to the exchequer college (Rammar Collegium a properly-closed ledger for the past year, with annexed vouchers of that part of the funds assigned for forest purposes which have been placed at the disposal of the administration, as well as of all other funds intrusted to the administration.

§ 17. Before the 1st of April every year the forest administration shall render to His Royal Majesty a tabular account of the cases which have been examined by the same, stating in this account upon whom the decision of the case depends at the end of the year.

§ 18. The forest administration shall also, before the 1st of October every year, render to His Royal Majesty a report for the past year of the state of the forest management, forest schools, and the chase, based upon not only the reports, accounts, and other informations which are transmitted from the officers at the forest corps and from the schools, but also upon the observations which the chief of the administration has made during his inspections, and which report shall contain, among other, a summary account of the charges preferred during the year by the officers and attendants of the forest corps for offenses against the forest and chase laws, as also every fifth year a synopsis of the reports of the last five years.

§ 19. The forest administration consists of a chief, a secretary, and a treasurer. At the administration may, in case of need, extraordinary officers be appointed as assistants.

§ 20. The forest administration will meet as often as required and the business to be discussed shall be laid before the chief either by the secretary or the treasurer, according to the distribution between them, as below stated, or, if there should be any doubt as to whom the laying before the chief of a certain case belongs, as the chief shall decide.

The chief shall alone decide, having learned the opinion of either or, if necessary, of both the secretary and the treasurer; and they may, if their opinions should differ, record the same, or they shall be considered having approved of the decision. On his official journeys the chief may, when he finds it necessary, order the enforcement of the law, as also give warning, and otherwise demand such security from the officer as the forest administration has to require. He shall, however, report the same to the forest administration, to be recorded at the next meeting which he shall attend.

During the absence of the chief on official journeys, or when he is legally prevented from attending to his office, the secretary and the treasurer shall jointly exercise the administration, being also jointly responsible for the decisions and measures upon which they agree. Should they be of different opinion, the opinion of the one reporting the case shall be the decisive one, and he alone shall be responsible for the same, provided the other has caused his opinion to be recorded.

The forest administration may not, during the absence of the chief, render annual reports, humble propositions for the filling of vacancies, give opinions in regard to appeals of cases decided in the presence of the chief, and in which the opinion of one or the other of the administration officers has differed, or in regard to new regulations or alterations of those existing; neither may the administration appoint or discharge officers or attendants, or alter existing rules, or stipulate new ones, should not the absence of the chief be so extended that steps must be taken before his return. A record shall be kept over each and every case which has been discussed. Letters and other documents shall be written and countersigned by the one who lays the matter before the administration, and who shall also dispatch and enter the same in the diary as soon as signed by the chief. In the absence of the chief the letters are signed by the secretary and the treasurer, "for the forest administration."

§ 21. The chief of the forest administration, who is responsible to His Royal Majesty for the fulfillment of the duties of the administration, and that the cases within their jurisdiction are properly decided and dispatched without delay, shall, with constant attention, see to that every one of the officers of the forest administration, with zeal and order, fulfill their duties, besides which he shall, by inspection-journeys in the country, ascertain the standing of the forest management, of the instruction at the schools, and of the chase, as well as how the officers of the forest corps and schools fulfill their respective duties; and he shall, when undertaking such journeys, which ought to be reported to His Royal Majesty, order an officer of the forest corps or schools to accompany him as secretary.

§ 22. The duties of the secretary are:

1. To examine documents and maps concerning surveys, and to lay before the administration all questions about the sanctioning or alteration of proposed plans of management, as well as to prepare and read all such cases which do not, according to the following section, belong to the treasurer;

2. To enter in the diary or journal of the administration all documents and maps, and to make out a table from the same and the dispatches of the administration;

3. To take care of the archives of the administration, and to give informations from the same, as well as to make extracts and copies of documents and maps kept at the same;

4. To keep a roll of the officers and attendants of the forest administration, forest corps, and schools; and

5. To exercise in the first hand the control the forest administration ought to exercise over the manner in which officers and attendants at the forest corps and the schools fulfill their duties, the reports of the faults or neglects he has observed, however, to be laid before the administration by the treasurer.

§ 23. The duties of the treasurer are:

1. To examine reports and accounts which, in accordance with § 13, shall be examined by the forest administration; the remarks he shall have cause to make shall, however, be laid before the administration by the secretary;

2. To examine all records of surveys and inspections of farms, manors, and localities assigned to the forest corps and schools, and to lay before the administration not only the remarks and projects he thereby has found reason to make, but also other questions concerning the management and care of the said farms;

3. To prepare and keep the ground-rent book mentioned in § 9;

4. To prepare and lay before the administration the projects for forest cultivation and similar works, with accompanying calculations of cost, which have been transmitted to the administration, as also to make out and report for examination the annual general projects for the use of the part of the forest funds placed at the disposal of the administration, in accordance with § 10;

5. Also to prepare and read the questions about the disposal or paying out of money belonging to the same part of the said funds;

6. To manage the economy of the administration and to take care of its movables; and

7. To make out and deliver to the administration, within the 1st of December every year, the ledger mentioned in § 16.

§ 24. The extra officers shall assist, by order of the chief, the secretary and the treasurer, in revisions, accounts, and chancery-work, as also in copying maps.

§ 25. The forest corps in the country consists of forest inspector as comptroller, district director as manager, and foresters as guards. The forest inspector is the chief of the officers within his district. Each district of a forest inspector is composed of several "riviers," each " rivier" being managed by a district director. The forester is the guard and the overseer over that part of the " rivier" which has been confided to him. When such are necessary, extra district directors may be appointed as assistants to serve within the " rivier," ou the responsibility of the ordinary ; also extra foresters may be appointed if required.

§ 26. The forest inspector shall superintend that his subordinates fulfill their duties zealously and carefully. He has not only to examine the quarterly and annual reports transmitted to him by the district directors, but also and particularly every year undertake inspection journeys to different parts of the district, in order to ascertain whether existing regulations or issued orders concerning the management of forest and chase are followed ; should in any way incorrectness, neglect, or misdemeanor have taken place, such must be corrected, and, besides, graver cases reported to the forest administration. The forest inspector shall, every year before the end of November, propose to the forest administration, and the latter decide, which forests shall be inspected by him during the coming year, it being the duty of the inspector to inspect during the year such public forests where there is a cause for such an inspection ; besides which, the station of every district director shall be inspected by the forest inspect or at least every third year and the schools within the district once a year.

§ 27. During the journeys of the forest inspector a record shall be kept, in which everything of consequence that has happened during the inspection journeys shall be entered, and this record shall, the journeys being finished for the year, be transmitted to the forest administration before the end of the following March.

§ 28. When the opinion of the forest inspector in regard to surveys, examination of surveys, or any other subject is requested, he shall, if necessary, before giving his opinion on the spot itself, ascertain the circumstances.

§ 29. The forest inspector is prohibited to, either himself or by other persons, survey forests belonging to private parties.

§ 30. It shall be the duty of the district director ("jägmästar ") to take proper care, according to existing regulations and approved plans of management or respectively-issued rules, of the crown-parks and quicksand fields which belong to the Crown, and re situated within the " rivier," as well as of the commons and forests belonging to the dwelling-places which are placed under the management of the forest corps, and to consequently himself arrange and lead the cultivation, felling, and all other work in the above-named forests, as well as to see that the guards properly exercise their functions. With regard to other public forests belonging to the " rivier," the district director shall superintend that approved plans of management are followed, or, when such plans are not made out, that the forests are used according to existing regulations ; he shall besides exercise necessary control over oak and timber trees which are not owned by private persons, as well as over other quicksand fields than those of which is spoken above, and also, in order to have a thorough idea of the state of all the forests within the " rivier," to procure, himself, necessary information about the private forests and their management.

§ 31. The district director shall, when ordered by the forest administration, survey the public forests for their proper management according to existing rules ; such a survey having been done, the district officer shall, observing what is stipulated in regard to remarks made by private persons, transmit to the forest administration for their approval a chart made as the survey with description of the plan of management and other documents ; he shall, besides, the case having been decided and ordered, alterations and additions having been entered upon the original chart and into the documents, again transmit to the forest administration the corrected copies, adding thereto, if the forest which has been surveyed is under the care of the district director, one, but, otherwise, two new copies of the chart, description, and plan of management. When any other than the district director of the "rivier" is ordered by the forest administration to make the survey, the appointed one has to observe what is stipulated for the district director in the foregoing paragraph. Of the copy of the chart, description, and plan of management returned from the forest administration, the district director shall take and transmit to the respective foresters a copy of each district, which wholly, or to a certain part, has been surveyed, and which copy shall embrace all that the foresters require to know.

§ 32. The district director shall also, in the manner now prescribed or in the future may be stipulated, revise the surveys which are to be held for the proper management of the common forests within the " rivier;" and the charts and descriptions made out at the survey shall be transmitted and corrected as above stipulated for the charts and descriptions of the district surveys.

§ 33. The district director shall diligently care for that forests and quicksand fields under his management, barren but intended to bear forests, become as soon as possible by proper means a woodland, observing in planting trees not to use any more expensive mode than is necessary for the purpose.

§ 34. When felling is to be done on public forests managed by the district director, or otherwise than for household purposes on other common forests, the district director shall himself mark the trees that may be felled and superintend the prescribed marking of the same. In stamping the trees, the foot of the trunk, as well as at a man's height, is provided with the crown-stamp, consisting of a royal crown, and below the same the two last ciphers of the year when the tree is marked; the stamp-iron, which is kept by the district director, shall never be used but in his presence.

§ 35. If crown-parks, quicksand fields belonging to the Crown upon which the community or private persons are entitled to fell trees, or if forests belonging to dwelling-places (official residences) which are managed by the district director, and where the dweller is entitled to wood for household purposes, are surveyed, the district director shall during the survey suitably mark out the trees which may be felled by the dweller or those entitled to fell trees and give them a list of the same free of charge. The district director shall also, where surveying a common, transmit, free of charge, a list of the trees which having been marked, are at the disposal of the administration of the common. Timber-trees intended for sale, and which are marked on crown-parks, quicksand fields belonging to the Crown, or on such forests, belonging to dwelling-places, the yield of which entirely or to a certain part shall go to the exchequer or the salary funds, shall during the survey be divided by the district director in certain lots, each separately numbered. The timber-trees already sold when being marked, which is the case with crown-parks and crown-lands in the læns of Kopparberg and Norrland, shall during the survey be suitably divided by the district director in separate tracts, which are assigned to the purchasers, thereby observing that, when several persons have purchased timber within the same tract, equal advantages as far as it is possible in regard to communication are given to the respective parties.

§ 36. All surveys necessary within the "rivier" shall also be so arranged by the district director that they are finished every year, if possible, before the 1st of October; and the time for each survey when made on account of the commune, or on forest from which the sale of timber will be made during the year, or already has been made for the account of the exchequer or the salary funds, shall by the care of the district director be published in the church of the parish or parishes within which the forest is situated, in the læns of Kopparberg and Norrland at least fourteen days, and in other parts of the kingdom at least eight days, before; but if any other common-forest is to be surveyed, shall the district director, within the time specified, inform the respective party who has requested the survey of the time for the same.

§ 37. In regard to proposing to His Royal Majesty's governor of province the marking of timber on crown-parks and crown-lands in the læns of Kopparberg and Norrland, it shall be the duty of the district director, with regard to his "rivier," to observe the regulations in the case stipulated for the respective forest officers. Again, in regard to crown-parks in other parts of the kingdom, quicksand fields belonging to the Crown, and the forests which belong to dwelling-places, the yield of which goes either altogether or to a certain part to the exchequer or the salary funds, the district director shall every year before the end of October—marking having been done—transmit to His Royal Majesty's governor of province an account of the timber which for the year may be sold from such forest; and this account, upon which His Royal Majesty's governor of the province shall base the publishing of the auction-sale, must be made out according to forms approved of by the forest administration, and besides contain the proposal of place and time for the sale. It shall also be the duty of the district director, in regard to the forests within the "rivier," mentioned in this section, with the exception of forests belonging to dwelling-places, managed by the dwellers, to annually, within the month of April, report to His Royal Majesty's governor of province the quality of grass or pasture which may be got from the said forests.

§ 38. The district director, or the officiating extra district director, or forester shall be present at the auction-sale of timber, grass, or pasture from the forests mentioned in this foregoing section, in order to give necessary information.

§ 39. Forest plants, seeds, and other similar forest products of less importance may, without injury to the forest, be taken from the same and sold by the district director managing the forest; he shall, however, respectively account for the returns. Unlawfully felled timber, which has been seized, shall be reported for sale to His Royal Majesty's governor of province. If the amount of such timber is small or difficult to guard until an auction of the same has taken place, through the care of His Royal Majesty's governor of province, the district director may request the nearest sheriff to sell the same.

§ 40. In regard to felling and carrying away of timber and other forest products sold

2 F C

from public forests, the district director shall, either in marking or otherwise, give such instructions which are necessary for the guarding or control of the same.

§ 41. The district director shall, every year, before the 1st of October, transmit to the forest administration two copies of a project to forest cultivation or other work, which ought to be done during the coming year, of forests managed by him, as well as a calculation of the cost of such work, for which cash is required.

§ 42. After the project and estimate mentioned in the foregoing section have been examined by the forest administration and the decision of the administration has been made known to the district director, the latter shall see that the works approved of by the forest administration are executed; and he shall, in regard to crown-parks within the "rivier" quicksand fields belonging to the Crown, and such forests which, belonging to dwelling-places, are managed by him, draw and receive in advance from the treasurer of the len, the funds necessary for these works, according to the regulations stipulated for this purpose by the forest administration.

§ 43. The district director shall, separately for each forest, account for not only the funds he shall receive toward the expenses for the care of the forests managed by him, or for other purposes, but also for all the forest products delivered from the said forests, as well as such forests belonging to the dwelling-places within the "rivier," which are not managed by him and of which a part of the income goes to the exchequer. The district director shall, therefore, according to the rules issued by the forest administration, keep requisite books, and every year, before the 1st of April, transmit to His Royal Majesty's governor of province proper accounts, based upon the same, for the past calendar year, these accounts to be accompanied by respective vouchers, and transmitted in two copies, with the exception of the accounts which embrace forest products delivered from such forests, of which either the whole or a part of the income shall go to the exchequer, of which only one copy is required, all timber to be entered by cubic foot, heavier timber by the piece, fuel and fencing in cords of 100 cubic feet or loads of 33½ cubic feet, and smaller timber in numbers of hundred and twenty.

§ 44. The district director shall, besides, with regard to such forests belonging to dwelling-places within the "rivier," which are not managed by him, and the greater or smaller part of the income of which goes to the exchequer or some salary funds, examine the accounts of the expenses for the management of such forests, and which accounts are transmitted to him by the respective owners of the forests.

§ 45. In regard to dwelling-places within the "rivier," assigned to foresters, the district director shall watch over that the same are, in regard to buildings and cultivation, properly managed and maintained.

§ 46. At the instance of His Royal Majesty's governor of the province, the district director shall assist at surveys and examination of dwelling-places and other public farms, and at explorations for ascertaining if surplus lands are suitable to be retained as crown-parks; also to explore quicksand fields in the order prescribed; besides which he shall, in order to guard the interest of the Crown at surveys and divisions, in regard to the selecting of land for crown-parks, be present at the meetings to which he shall for this purpose be called by the respective surveyor. The district director shall also, with regard to business belonging to his office, give his opinion whenever requested by His Royal Majesty's governor of province.

§ 47. The district director shall, when felling is more extensively done than permitted on commons managed by the owners themselves, or where, on such as other common forest within the "rivier," not managed by the district director, the regulations for the guarding and care of the forest stipulated in the approved plan of management are not respectively observed, report the case to His Royal Majesty's governor of province, provided the forest does not belong to the farm of a public institution, the ownership of which is not yet legalized, in which case the report of the district director ought to be made, if the farm to which the forest belongs is cultivated by the lessee, to the authority under whom it is subordinate, but otherwise to the forest administration, it being the duty of the latter authority, the report having been made, to call attention to the case of the managers of the institution. Should the dweller, settler, or lessee of a public farm or locality exceed his lawful right in regard to the use of the forest, or should any offense be committed against the forest and hunting laws, which not only should infringe upon the right of private parties, the district director shall prefer charges against the offender.

§ 48. At the end of every quarter, and within one month, the district director shall report to the forest inspector all that has taken place within his district during the passed quarter; also the inspection journeys and surveys which have been made during this time within the district, either by himself or appointed extra district directors; more important events, as large fires and damages by storm, &c., ought, however, to be immediately reported.

§ 49. The district director shall also, every year before the 1st of April, transmit to the forest administration a report of everything worth remarking in regard to the management of the forest and chase that has taken place during the past year; this report, of which the district director shall deliver a copy to the forest inspector of the district within the time above mentioned, ought to embrace, not only an account of the work which has been done during the year in the forests managed by the district director, but also information about the influence former measures have exercised and how other common forests within the district are managed; the report ought, besides, to contain a list of all charges preferred during the year through the care of the district director for offenses against the forest and hunting laws.

§ 50. It shall be the duty of the forester ("krono jägaren") to see to it that division lines and other boundaries around the common forests, over which he has been ordered to watch, are kept open and undisturbed, and also to report to the district director all unlawful felling and hunting, and to exert himself in finding the offender and to prove his guilt.

§ 51. In forest cultivation, felling, carrying away of timber, and in other works in the forest belonging to his district, the forester shall superintend that the orders of the district director are properly observed and that the work is carefully done; he shall also take care of the planting "schools" laid out within the said forests.

§ 52. The forester shall carefully superintend that felled or only marked forest product within his district are not wrongfully taken away; and he shall ask the owner, when carrying away his timber, to give him a receipt, which he will hand to the district director.

§ 53. The forest inspector and the district director shall each keep a list of all official papers received as well as a copy-book for official letters sent; they shall also, as well as the forester, take proper care of all maps and documents belonging to the office. At the change of officers an inventory ought to be made to the forester by the district director, to the district director by the forest inspector, and to the latter by a person appointed by the forest administration.

§ 54. At occurring fires, the respective district director and foresters shall immediately, on being acquainted of the fact, set out for the place of the fire and take suitable measures for the extinguishing of the fire; the district director shall take the command of the firemen.

§ 55. The district director and foresters shall endeavor to destroy voracious and noxious animals, and to promote a proper hunting.

§ 56. Officers belonging to the forest corps shall, except on special permission of the forest administration, live within their respective districts, and at the dwelling-places, where such suitably built are assigned to the officers.

§ 57. Each and every one of the officers and attendants of the forest corps shall obey the orders of their respective superiors.

§ 58. In order to be competent to the office of secretary or treasurer at the forest administration, and as forest inspector, and district director, the applicant shall have graduated from the Forest Institute. No other but those who have graduated from the Forest Institute can be appointed extra officers at the forest administration or extra district directors. Those who have graduated from public forest schools or proved themselves to be competent to the position shall be appointed foresters in preference to other applicants.

§ 59. The chief of the forest administration, the secretary, and the treasurer at the same, and the district director are appointed by His Royal Majesty. The vacancy of the secretary, treasury, or district directorship is published by the forest administration three times in the Post och Inrikes Tidningar, where, after applicants may, within fifty-six days from the time of the vacancy, tender their humble applications, accompanied by merit list and certificates to the forest administration, who, according to stipulated rules, will transmit to His Royal Majesy their proposition to the filling of the vacancy, as well as the applications. The forest inspector is appointed for a certain time by His Royal Majesty upon the proposal of the forest administration. Extraordinary officers of the forest administration and extra district directors are nominated by the administration after the opinion of the district director has been learned. The administration nominates their attendants and foresters after the proposal of the district director of the rivier. The district director shall, as soon as a place is vacant, engage a suitable person until the nomination of the forest administration has been issued.

§ 60. The chief of the forest administration may, business permitting, enjoy leave of absence twice a year, each time for a period of fourteen days, after having reported his intended absence to the royal department of the finances, and the secretary and the treasurer may, with the consent of the chief, obtain leave of absence for one month, once a year, however, not when the chief is absent.

The forest administration may grant the forest inspector and the district director leave of absence for a time not exceeding three months. Leave of absence for longer time may be applied for to His Royal Majesty; the application of the secretary, treasurer, forest inspector or district director, to be delivered to the forest administration, who, approvingly or disapprovingly, transmit the same to His Royal Majesty. Leave of absence for a longer or shorter time may be granted by the administration to extra ordinary officers and attendants at the forest administration as well as to extra district directors and foresters; however, leave of absence for a time not exceeding fourteen days may be granted by the district director of the rivier to extra district directors and foresters. Officers at the forest administration are not allowed to stay, without leave of absence, outside their districts for longer time than three days; foresters may not, without the permission of the district directors, remain outside their district for more than one day.

§ 61. When leave of absence is granted by His Royal Majesty to the secretary, treasurer, forest inspector or the district director, His Royal Majesty will, upon the proposal of the forest administration, prescribe how the office shall in the mean time be attended to; but should there be any vacancy among the officers or attendants belonging to the forest administration, the forest corps or schools, the forest administration will see to the temporary filling of the same.

§ 62. If an office at the forest corps to which a dwelling-place is assigned should be vacant by death, discharge, or promotion, after the 14th of March, and before Thomas day, he or his heirs will give up the dwelling-place to next following 14th of March, but if after Thomas day on the 14th of March after the elapse of one year from Thomas day ; in both cases shall the new appointee compensate his predecessor for the standing crops, and remunerate him for such works as have been done in preparing for a crop. Foresters will, as soon as nominated, take possession of their dwelling-places.

§ 63. Should the chief of the forest administration make himself liable to any faults or neglect in the service, charges will be preferred against him at the supreme court of His Royal Majesty and the Kingdom, and if such be the case with the secretary or the treasurer, the chief may, if such be necessary, dismiss them for the time the suit shall last. Extra officers at the forest administration, who shall make himself guilty of fault or neglect in the service, may receive warning from the administration; or if he continues his offenses, he shall be dismissed from office either for a certain time or forever. Attendant at the administration who is unreliable or disobedient, may, according to circumstances, either receive warning from the administration, lose his situation for a certain time, or be discharged.

§ 64. Should the forest inspector or district director neglect through carelessness, omit or refuse to fulfill his duties, or should he stay away from his office without permission or legal cause, he will receive warning of the forest administration; should he continue his offenses, he will be fined to an amount corresponding to not above three months' salary, or dismissed from office for an equal time ; should he, however, commit similar offenses, or be guilty of graver neglect, a public accuser, appointed by His Royal Majesty's governor of province, will, at the request of the forest administration, prefer charges against him at the respective court, and the forest administration will in such a case, or when charges are preferred against officers at the forest corps, dismiss the person from office, when circumstances so require. Should the extra district director neglect his duties, the stipulations in the foregoing section in regard to extra ordinary officers at the forest administration may be applied. Foresters found to be incompetent, careless, or neglectful, or guilty of unfaithfulness, partiality or selfishness may, having previously received warning of the respective district director, without changing his conduct, be dismissed by the forest administration for a certain time, or discharged.

§ 65. Should an officer at the forest corps fail to render, within the time specified, the information, declaration, or account required by the forest administration, the administration will, for each repeated neglect, fix a suitable fine for the exceeding time.

§ 66. No complaint can be made of received warning, but from the decision of the forest administration, by whom the offender is sentenced to other punishment, may humble appeal be made, which will have to be transmitted to His Royal Majesty through his department of finances, within the time specified in the royal instruction of December 14, 1866.

§ 67. Concerning the business of the forest administration with regard to the filling of vacancies at the forest institute and forest schools, or in regard to leave of absence applied for by officers and attendants at the same, the rules stipulated above for district directors will exist in regard to the manager of the forest institute and the teacher at the same, and at the other schools ; the same regulations exist for overseers and attendants at the schools as for foresters.

§ 68. This instruction shall be in force from the commencement of the next year, 1870, when the royal instruction of the 16th of March, 1838, for the forest and chase corps, shall cease to be valid.

Which all whom it may concern shall have to obey.

In witness whereof we have hereunto set our hand and caused our royal seal to be affixed.

The Palace at Stockholm, November 19, 1869.

CARL. [L. S.]

GUST OF UGGLAS.

[Translation from the Swedish.]

3. *His Majesty the King's gracious regulations for forest instruction within the Kingdom, given at the Palace of Stockholm, May 25, 1860.*

We, Charles, by the Grace of God the King of Sweden, Norway, &c., &c., make known: That, whereas the rules for the forest institute, graciously given on the 15th of October, 1828, in several regards require some amendment, and whereas it has been lately decided to establish, at the expense of the government, lower forest schools, we have found proper, having learned the humble opinion of our administration of forests, to cancel the above-mentioned rules, and hereby graciously to order that free instruction shall be given at the forest schools, which stand under the administration of forests, at the forest institute, in a higher course of teaching, for the education of forest managers, and at the forest schools in a lower course, for the education of skillful foresters and planters, and we do, for these schools, and the private forest education, supported by public funds, graciously sanction the following regulations:

CHAPTER I.

THE FOREST INSTITUTE—ITS OBJECT AND ORGANIZATION.

§ 1. A suitable locality in the royal park, near Stockholm, shall continue to be placed to the disposal of the forest institute, embracing lecture-rooms, library, rooms for collections, the director, one teacher and one porter, also necessary ground for nursery, tree-planting, and target-ground; a suitable forest in the vicinity of the city shall also be placed under the regular care and management of the institute, in order to impart to the pupils practical knowledge herein.

§ 2. In order to teach the pupils surveying, appraisement, and the technical terms of the forest, they shall, during a certain time every year, be employed in forests suitable for the purpose, under the direction of the teachers; separate funds will be assigned for this purpose.

§ 3. To assist the pupils during their stay at the institute, a certain number of stipends, the amount of which will be separately fixed, will be assigned to such indigent pupils who have made themselves deserving of the same, through industry, skill, and good conduct.

§ 4. The institute is to be managed by a director, appointed by His Royal Majesty, and the director, together with four teachers, also appointed by His Royal Majesty, will furnish the instruction, viz: one the care and management of forests, one hunting and forest laws, one natural history, and one mathematics; these teachers will be entitled to their years of service, as merits equal to the forest and chase officers of the kingdom, the two latter only in case they have graduated at the forest institute. For the appointing of director, as well as teachers, the forest administration will nominate candidates. At the institute is also a porter, appointed by the director, and may by him be removed.

§ 5. The course of instruction shall embrace mathematics and natural history to the extent required for the superintendence of forests and the chase; knowledge of the regulations for the forest and the chase, book-keeping, and of the forms for forest accounts; hunting; theoretical and practical knowledge of forest-appraisement; cultivation of woods and forest-technology; as well as expertness in surveying, map-drawing, leveling and shooting.

§ 6. The course of instruction will be continued during two years, counted from the commencement of the month of June every year, and be so arranged that fully educated pupils may yearly graduate and new ones be admitted in their place.

§ 7. Pupils who wish to obtain certificates of having graduated, shall, having previously undergone a probation at a public examination, manifest sufficient knowledge and skill in all the branches which they have been taught at the institute. In order to obtain a certificate for forest-management, the pupil shall prove himself to have satisfactorily constructed a map, with regular plan of forest surveying and cultivation.

§ 8. The instruction shall continue during the whole year, with the exception of three weeks' vacation during Christmas, and one week after the yearly examination, and shall be thus regulated, that the pupils acquire, from commencement of October until the end of May, theoretical and such practical knowledge as local circumstances at the institute admit of, and that, during the summer months, the pupils are occupied in the forests of the government, and under the direction of the teachers, with surveying and estimation of forests, and with the most usual modes of the cultivation, care, and felling of trees.

§ 9. Every year, at the commencement of the month of June, the pupils shall be publicly examined in all the subjects in which they have received instruction. The pupil who, having previously undergone a probation, proves himself at the examination to possess the knowledge and skill mentioned in § 7, may, without regard to the longer or shorter time he has been at the college, receive due certificate.

THE DIRECTOR OF THE FOREST INSTITUTE.

§ 10. The director ought to have made himself known as possessing knowledge and experience of forest-managing, and shall live within the locality of the institute, in order to properly exercise his functions. His duties shall embrace not only the administration of the institute and the responsibility of its operations, and of the completeness of the instruction, but also to promote the development of and spread throughout the country the science of forest-management.

It shall consequently be the duty of the director—

1. To quarterly collect from the treasury of His Royal Majesty and the realm, at the request of the forest administration, the funds assigned to salaries and maintenance of the institute; to dispose of these funds according to regulations, and for each calendar year account for their disposal, which account shall be delivered before the end of the next following February to the forest administration for auditing.

2. To watch over the care and maintenance of the ground, buildings, nurseries, archives, library, collections, tools, implements, and other movables of the institute, and to see to it that complete lists of the same are made out and always at hand. He shall, however, according to what is stated below, have right to suitably distribute between the teachers the administration and care of collections, tools, and the movables.

3. To, having examined the certificates produced and the amount of knowledge possessed by the candidates for admission, admit them as pupils, and, according to statements of the teachers, separately for each branch, issue certificates to pupils who have finished their course, and to propose to the forest administration the distribution of the assigned stipends among such pupils who shall be considered most deserving of the same.

4. To issue regulations as well for the maintenance of good order and morality within the institute as for the suitable course of teaching and the manner of imparting the same, for which purpose the director shall make out a regular table of instruction, so that the business be properly distributed between the teachers, and the time advantageously employed to the benefit of the pupils.

5. To himself instruct in one of the head branches of forest economy as well as, business permitting, be present at the preliminary examination of the pupils in the other branches.

6. To endeavor in every possible manner to promote the knowledge and spread of an improved forest economy and management of the chase within the kingdom, for the purpose of which he must keep himself informed of the progress of the science and technical terms of the forest, even in foreign countries, and to write and publish pamphlets on the subject whenever circumstances require.

7. To report on the forest administration partly such business which requires the decision of His Royal Majesty, and partly such steps in regard to an improved forest economy and management of the chase within the kingdom which may be found necessary.

8. To make such reports or give such information concerning the forest economy and the management of the chase which the forest administration may demand, as well as to render to the same yearly accounts of the operations of the institute; and—

9. To give the porter instructions in regard to his attendance and other duties at the institute.

THE TEACHERS AT THE FOREST INSTITUTE.

§ 11. The teacher of forest economy ought to have graduated at the institute with honors, and thereafter, on his own responsibility, manage a forest district, and, as his services are constantly required, he ought to live within the institute. This teacher shall—

1. Instruct and examine in all the branches of forest economy in which the director himself does not teach, and, besides, practically instruct the pupils in surveying and estimating of the area of forests, and the cubic contents of trees, construction of maps, valuation of soil, growing and felled timber, to collect and preserve seeds, the laying-out and care of nurseries, forest growing and planting, the position of seed-trees, clearing, to quench quicksand, felling of trees, assorting and marking of timber, as well as to conduct a party of the pupils in the forests for practical measuring, estimating, and dividing of forest land.

2. To have under his care, and to account for, the archives, library, and movables of the institute, with the exception of those for which the teacher of the chase and regulations is responsible.

3. To manage the economy of and account for the forests assigned to the care of the institute.

4. To assist the director in watching over that given instructions are followed, and in maintaining industry and order among the pupils; and

5. To take command of the place in the absence of the director.

§ 12. The teacher of the chase and regulations shall have graduated at the institute with honors, and thereafter served at the forest and chase corps of the Kingdom. This teacher shall—

1. Instruct and examine in the knowledge of fire-arms, shooting, the theory and technical terms of the chase, forest and chase regulations, and book-keeping.

2. Assist at the practices in forest economy, and conduct, during the summer season, a party of the pupils on practical measuring, estimating, and dividing of forest land.

3. To exercise the pupils in target-practice, and also, when there is an opportunity of hunting and driving game, instruct the pupils in the care of wolf-pits, traps, nets, and cages; the making and care of hunting implements; the keeping of forests, as well as to prefer charges against poachers and other offenders against game and forest laws; and—

4. To take care of and account for the tools and collections of models of the institute, as well as of the forest and hunting implements, and of what belongs to the target-ground.

§ 13. The teacher of natural history ought to have made himself known as thoroughly well acquainted with this science. His duties shall be—

1. To instruct and examine in those parts of physics, chemistry, and mineralogy which are required for the knowledge of forest climate and soil, in general and forest botany, and in zoology, as far as this branch of knowledge is connected with the forests.

2. To instruct in the manner of preparing herbaria, and of stuffing and preserving animals and insects.

3. To conduct the pupils on mineralogical and botanical excursions, and to practice with them the examining of soil and plants.

4. To instruct the pupils during visits to the museum of the Academy of Sciences; and

5. To take care of and account for the zoological and botanical collections of the institute, and to make out complete lists of the same.

§ 14. The teacher of mathematics ought to have made himself known as thoroughly acquainted with this science. This teacher shall instruct and examine in arithmetic, algebra, planimetry, stereometry, trigonometry, conical sections, geometrical constructions, descriptive geometry, general and forest architecture, elements of mechanics, and theory of the construction and use of mathematical instruments. He shall besides practice with the pupils the drawing and copying of maps, calculating of areas, sketching maps, surveying, construction of buildings and roads for forest purposes, with estimates of materials and labor, measuring of cubic contents, and adjustment of instruments.

PUPILS AT THE FOREST INSTITUTE.

§ 15. In order to be admitted at the forest institute, application shall be made to the director within the middle of the month of May, and the following certificates annexed to the same:

That the applicant is at least 18 and not above 24 years old; that his constitution is good and faultless, and not affected with any kind of incurable disease; that he has always conducted himself well; that he either has passed such examination and obtained certificates of approval in mathematics, natural history, and Swedish grammar, which entitles him to enter the universities of the Kingdom; or that he has been examined by the appointed teachers at any of the elementary schools within the kingdom in each of these branches, and found to possess sufficient knowledge therein to enable him to graduate from the school; also, that he has, during at least one year, with some forester practiced and acquired sufficient skill in the economy and surveying of the forest.

§ 16. Applicants whose applications are complete, and who consequently may expect to fill the vacancies at the institute, must publicly and in the presence of the director be examined by the teachers in arithmetic and algebra, planimetry and stereometry, general botanics, and zoology; also, to write a Swedish theme.

§ 17. Those exhibiting the greatest knowledge shall have the preference of being admitted to the institute.

§ 18. At the commencement of every year the director shall propose to the forest administration for receiving of stipends those of the pupils who are in need of assistance, and have shown themselves most deserving of same through industry, skill, and orderly conduct.

§ 19. The pupils shall obey the orders of the director and the teachers, orderly and decently conduct themselves, follow the regulations at the institute, and attentively and industriously profit by the instructions.

§ 20. Should the pupil disobey the orders of the director or the teachers, create any disturbance at the institute, conduct himself in a disorderly manner, or neglect his studies, he shall receive warning from the director. Should he not then change his conduct, but continue his offenses, the director shall, after having consulted the teachers, send him away from the institute.

CHAPTER II.

THE FOREST SCHOOLS—THEIR OBJECT AND ORGANIZATION.

§ 21. Suitable localities, large enough to permit both teachers and pupils to live there, shall be placed to the disposal of the forest schools at such places as will be especially determined upon.

§ 22. To a certain number of pupils, unable to maintain themselves at the school, sufficient assistance shall be given, according to what is therefor specially prescribed.

§ 23. The forest schools shall be managed, under the superintendence of the nearest district director of forests, by a teacher appointed by His Royal Majesty the King, after having been proposed to the situation by the govenor of the province and with the approval of the forest administration; this teacher shall be assisted by a ranger, nominated by the forest administration.

§ 24. The instruction at the forest school shall embrace the four first rules of arithmetic and the rules of proportion in whole and decimal numbers; knowledge of scales for plan-drawings, as far as required for making of maps and measuring distances; knowledge of square and cubic measures with practical application at the measuring of the extent and content of surfaces and solid bodies; knowledge of the nourishing organs of the forest trees and of their food, and the natural conditions for their thriving; knowledge of the most dangerous insects of the Swedish forest, and of the manner of destroying them; the chief principles of rational forest economy, and knowledge of the rules existing for the peace and keeping of forests, marking and carrying of timber, hunting, and also of the legal form for entering charges. The pupils will also be practiced in marking out and measuring of forest-lines; tilling places, and sowing fields; calculating of the cubic content of trees and timber; the position of seed-trees; sowing for hand and planting as well as the preparing of the soil for forest-growing; collecting and assorting of forest-seeds; clearing and cutting, assorting and piling of timber; marking cattle and making out of grazing-lists; laying up and keeping patrol-lists; making out lists of unlawfully-felled timber on which embargo has been laid; monthly reports and service accounts; the trapping of beasts, and the grand chase.

§ 25. The course of instruction shall begin on the 1st of October every year and continue until the middle of the following June, during which time all the respective subjects and exercises shall have been taught to the pupils, whereafter they are publicly examined in the presence of the district director in order to ascertain the knowledge and skill they have acquired.

§ 26. The pupil who has satisfactorily passed the examination is entitled to receive certificate of approved skill, issued by the district director and the principal of the school.

THE TEACHER OF THE SCHOOL.

§ 27. For the competency as teacher at the forest school, which office entitles him to count as many years of service within the forest and chase corps, the applicant shall have graduated at the forest institute and received certificate of approved knowledge, besides having been forest-manager on his own responsibility. This teacher is the chief in command at the place, the principal of the school, and accounts for and is responsible for the proper management of the school. He shall, consequently, quarterly, receive the funds assigned to the school, use them with judgment, and yearly account for the same, which account shall, within the time specified in §10, mom. 1, for the forest institute and for the object mentioned in the said mom, be forwarded to the forest administration through the governor of the province. It shall, besides, be his duty to arrange the teaching and exercises to the benefit of the pupils; to keep good order and decent conduct within the school; to impart himself the theoretical knowledge, and to superintend and correct the exercises and work in the forest. He shall also render yearly report over the operations of the school, which is forwarded to the forest administration through the governor of the province.

"SKOGSRÄTTAREN," OR ASSISTANT.

§ 28. The assistant must have made himself known as steadily and orderly, to be able to write, and well acquainted with all kind of forest-works. He is subordinate to the direct command of the teacher; he has the care of all the implements and materials of the school, for which he is responsible and shall account for to the teacher; manages the school in the absence of the teacher, and is responsible that the exercises and works are properly done, and assists in keeping good order among the pupils.

THE PUPILS OF THE FOREST SCHOOL.

§ 29. Those wishing to be admitted to the forest school shall make their application to the principal in their own handwriting, with annexed respective certificate of a clergyman, of good conduct, and of good and faultless bodily constitution, and if the applicant has been in service, a service certificate; the applicant shall be able to read fluently Swedish and Latin letters and writing, write an intelligible hand, know the first four rules of arithmetic, and be from twenty to thirty years old.

§ 30. Having examined the applications and the applicants, the principal of the school shall admit as pupils the most skillful and best conducted.

§ 31. The pupils shall obey the orders and prescriptions of the teacher and assistant, and observe industry, order, and good conduct. Should the pupil disobey the teacher, or the assistant disobey the rules of the school, be neglectful or disorderly in his conduct, or should he create disturbance, he shall receive warning of the principal ; should he not then change his conduct, but continue his offenses, the principal shall send him away from the school.

CHAPTER III.

PRIVATE FOREST-INSTRUCTION.

§ 32. To the establishing of forest schools in the respective provinces of the kingdom, and to the education of competent assistants at the managing of private forests, His Royal Majesty and the government will, yearly, contribute as far as the funds will permit and His Royal Majesty shall deem requisite, provided the communities which apply for such an assistance shall fulfill the following conditions :

1. That the community shall place requisite locality to the disposal of the school, furnish the teacher as well as the pupils with apartments, and pay for the maintenance of the school.

2. That the organization of the school and the proposed rules for its operations has been sanctioned by His Royal Majesty ; and,

3. That the operations of the school, of which a yearly report shall be made to the forest administration, shall be exercised under the superintendence of the nearest district director and the forest administration.

In regard to the time for applying for the positions as director, teacher, and assistant, and for resignations, how leave of absence shall be applied for or charges preferred for offense and neglect in service, as well as the punishment therefor, the regulations prescribed in the instructions for the forest administration shall be in force.

All of which whom it may concern shall obey.

In witness whereof we have hereunto set our hand and caused our royal seal to be affixed.

The Palace at Stockholm, May 25, 1860.

CARL. [L. S.]

J. A. GRIPENSTEDT.

[Translation from the Swedish.]

4. *Circular of the royal administration of forests to all employés in the "forest corps" and forest instruction, concerning principles for the division of the public forests for the purpose of systematic economy. Given June 29, 1867.*

1. The dividing or allotment of a forest consists in its delineation on a map with description and economical plan based on careful estimates having a view to the future of the forest and the highest reasonable income that can be derived from it.

2. The allotting is effected so that there may be introduced, as circumstances require, high-forest culture with tract-cutting or systematic thinning, or, nevertheless, for applying low-forest culture.

3. Forest is divided, according to its extent and nature, into more or less blocks. Smaller forests however may each comprise only a single block. The block is divided into divisions or parcels, whose limits are generally determined by natural formation or permanent marks, and these again into subdivisions, including differences which have been observed in surveying, delineating, and estimating the forest.

4. In the surveying is noted only such differences of the forest best and ground as, according to the above-mentioned method of forest work, exercise some influence thereon : and with the objects and differences noted at the surveying shall be added on the map the boundaries exactly to correspond with the facts. When a correct map happens to have been previously drawn up, a copy of it, with requisite additions, shall be used in the allotment of the forest.

5. The map of the forest shall be drawn up on such scale as allows requisite clearness in specifying what should be noted thereon for the economy of the forest.

6. The forest is estimated in cubic feet or in cords of 100 cubic feet (Swedish) solid measure, except when the allotment or dividing takes place for thinning, (applicable

to heavy timber,) when the estimate is made by number or piece. The estimate ought, as near as possible, to correspond with the reality, but had better be too low than too high.

7. The description shall include all important matters which, at the execution of the allotment, can be of weight for the economy of the forest.

8. The plan of management is drawn up for a period of twenty years and ought to include the requisite prescriptions as to the manner of working the forest, rotation time, consumption, culture, and the other means of administration which have not already been prescribed by the public statutes.

9. Tract-cutting will have the preference, as a manner of working the forest, except where from local circumstances it is unsuitable.

10. The rotation period should be extended as far as is necessary for raising the different sorts of trees and forest production which are counted on from the forest, but without occasioning such delay in consumption that any part of the forest shall thereby receive injury or deteriorate in value.

11. The estimate of what shall be consumed during the period of division or allotment shall be based on the forest's growth, the extent of ground, and on the known quantity of wood and timber, ascertained by careful calculation, whereof no more may be taken out than corresponds with the growth of the forest during the said time.

12. During the last year of the division period a revision is made for searching out the changes the forest has undergone and for drawing up the economy plan for the following division period.

Moreover, the government having authorized the administration of forests to issue regulations which may be required in conformity with the above principles, the administration of forests has found it reasonable to ordain as follows:

1. The method of working a forest, mentioned in paragraph 2, above, can, where necessary, be introduced on the same block, though on separate parts thereof; for example, forest-grown rocky hills, moss tracts, or other land on which systematic thinning seems an object, also such tracts as seem suitable for low-forest culture, may enter into the same plan of economy with tract-cutting, where the grounds have not sufficient extent for more than one block.

2. In dividing the forest into blocks, regard is had that as far as possible the older, middle-aged, and young forest "bestands" are in suitable relations to each other, also that the block obtains a proper form. The ground allotted in the block for tract-cutting may not exceed "6,000 quadrat ref." (1.305 acres.) With the introducing of systematic heavy-timber thinning, block allotment is fixed according to the means for floating, and accordingly a connected forest of even 12,000 acres may be reckoned to a block, providing the product therefrom can be floated on the same water-course. Lands whereon low-forest culture is introduced, and which are not entered in the economy plan that has been fixed for tract-cutting, are divided into blocks of at most 1200 acres. When blocks are not situated apart they ought to have natural boundaries, as water-courses, marsh, and rocky-hill extents, &c., &c., or nevertheless be bounded by highways or fences; but if such do not exist, they are separated by means of a line cleared through the forest to the width of 20 feet.

3. In dividing the block into parcels or divisions, the principal object of which is to facilitate "orienting" or astronomical directions, and clearness in description, likewise attaining an approximating homogeneous forest bestand, the same is to be observed concerning their boundaries that has just been mentioned in respect to blocks; nevertheless the separating lines may be cleared only the width of 10 feet. The forest land of a division should not exceed 200 acres except in forests which are allotted for merchantable or heavy timber, within which, as comprising the division or parcel, may be reckoned only those parts divided by natural boundaries. Connected forest-blocks of 200 acres extent, or less, constitute only a division or parcel.

4. The surveying of the forest, where it is so required, may be based, as heretofore, on parallel lines running in right angles, or over valleys and summit extents in oblique direction: nevertheless hereafter these lines ought not to be cut or cleared more than is necessary for making them visible, but shall instead be blazed to a breadth of ten feet. In the allotment of the forest for the purpose of systematic heavy-timber thinning, smaller impediments, unless sketched on the map, shall only be noted in the description.

5. Forest maps shall be drawn up on a scale of $\frac{1}{8000}$ of natural size, with these exceptions: lands allotted for heavy-timber thinning shall be mapped on a scale of $\frac{1}{20000}$ of natural size; lands for low-forest culture, according to separate plan of economy, shall be mapped on a scale of $\frac{1}{4000}$ of natural size. A separate map is drawn up for each block. On the just-mentioned maps of $\frac{1}{20000}$ scale, two or three blocks may nevertheless be contained, according to circumstances. When the forest is composed of several blocks, with map for each, a comprehensive map of the whole forest may be prepared, showing the relative situation of the blocks, on a scale of $\frac{1}{20000}$ of natural size; and with heavy-timber thinning $\frac{1}{50000}$ of natural size. The map of the floating-courses, below mentioned, are drawn on a scale of $\frac{1}{50000}$ of natural size. When a comprehen-

sive map on the scale aforementioned has been prepared, the floating-courses should be shown thereon, and in such case no separate map of these is needed. The maps shall be well and plainly drawn, colored, provided with names of bordering estates, forests, or the like, written around, title, scale, and north direction whereon the variation is observed. The cleared or blazed lines and the separating lines pertaining to the project for period allotment or division shall be drawn on the map, also the yearly clearing or cutting bounds in the first period; the latter, nevertheless, only on maps of forests which are not under the immediate administration of the forest establishment.

6. The valuation or estimate of the forest is undertaken in conformity with the recognized principles of forest science separately for each subdivision, with regard to differences of ground and forest bestand.

7. The description consists of general and bestand description.

8. The general description is based in certain parts on bestand description, and shall under separate titles account for—

History of the changes which the forest has undergone financially, state and administration of possessory right, wherewith, if practicable, the official proceedings may be introduced on which the changes or improvements have been based and the influence of these, of forest fires, of injuries by storms and the like on the forest's present condition.

The uses or service with which the forest, from one cause or another, is charged; how far these are based on culture or resolutions, and in the latter case what, also, the influence on the forest which the uses produce.

Boundaries on adjoining stranger owners; also, when the forest belongs to homestead or farm, on the thereto belonging arable and pasture land; wherewith for that case any land which did not before belong to the forest, but which is included in the allotment, with the reason therefor, ought separately to be given, regard being had to what is prescribed in Royal Forest Regulations of the 29th June, 1866, section 38.

Nature of the forest land, nature of the forest bestand in general, according to bestand description.

Block allotment or dividing, and motives for the same.

Prevailing winds, and their effect.

Depredations and wastes: to what extent the forest is exposed to such, and their nature.

Watching or care; how this is ordered, and how far sufficient.

Pasture and autumn-mowing, and what effect such use has on the forest.

Selling of the produce of the forest, where this can come in question, wherewith, when this is dependent on opportunity of floating, a map of the floating-course in the forest and in its neighborhood is annexed, providing such map can be had without separate survey.

With several other relations which, in and for the forest administration, can be of weight, which like the above-mentioned ought to be stated under separate titles.

9. THE DESCRIPTION OF THE BESTAND.—Table No. 1, 1, which is prepared in tabular form, and which, with the exception of area reports, composed in proportion to the progress of the survey and valuation, contains the following columns:

1. *Division*, or parcel, (in the Swedish "skiften,") wherein is introduced the name of the division, in what block it has been divided, also the letters whereby these are denoted on the map.

2. *Subdivision*, in which column is placed the letter whereby the differences of the forest land and forest bestand have been denoted on the map.

3. *Extent*, wherein the area is given in new measuring, (quadrat ref and quadrate poles,) and which column is subdivided in two, namely:

a. *Forest land*, where regard is had to the area of forest-bearing ground, the subdivisions are given as—

α. *Forest-grown*, or—

β. *Bare*, under which latter designation may be introduced as well such land as produces only bushes and scattered trees as that which shall be cleared, during the division period for effecting satisfactory re-growth; also—

b. *Impediments and land not regarded sufficiently fertile for forests*, under which is noted such rocky hills, marshes, mosses, &c., which cannot be counted on to bear forest; also such preventing sand-holes, ways, and tilled places, &c., whereon forest will not be grown.

4. *Land* where under the subdivision is described with regard to the quality of the land and soil.

5. *Situation*, where the situation is described as well with regard to moisture as in relation to prevailing winds.

6. *The forest*, which column is subdivided into four:

a. *Sort of trees*, wherein is introduced the kind of trees the forest bestands consist of, with special remarks as to the prevailing—

b. *Growth, closeness, windfalls, previous treatment*, &c., where a fuller description of the forest bestand is given, as well as how the same seems to have been treated previously.

c. Amount of production, wherein is noted the number of cords, at 100 cubic feet (Swedish) solid measure, which the growing forest contains.

a. By quadrat ref (say 10,000 square feet) in whole and tenths of cords, and—

3. By subdivision in whole cords; or nevertheless with heavy or merchantable timberthinning number of sticks per quadrat ref and in the whole subdivision ; also—

d. Age class, wherein is introduced the prevailing ages of the forest-bestand, designed to show twenty-year-age classes, from 1–20, 20–40, 40–60 years, &c., whereafter, under the title of *treatment of the bestand during the division period.* (Table No. 1, 2,) follows :

7. *Manner of working the forest*, in which column is noted how far the bestand shall proceed under allotment of tract-cutting, or if thinning or low-forest culture should be there introduced ; and—

8. *Special means*, including accounts of what ought to be adopted for the bestand and land during the time for which the division is regarded to be effective, whereto shall be stated for the occurrence of help-pruning or preparatory clearing (or cutting) that amount of wood and timber which thereby, according to valuation, it is considered can be obtained per quadrat ref. The area as well as quantity of wood and timber on the subdivisions may be summed up for every division or parcel, and a compendium introduced at the end of the table, wherein the whole of the area of the division or parcel and quantity of wood and timber noted shows the extent and bulk of the wood and timber, as well as a like compendium for the separate blocks to show the whole area of the forest and stock of wood in cords, or with heavy or merchantable timber-thinning, in timber.

To the description of the bestand belong, equally with tract-cutting, a compendium of the area which the different age-classes occupy, and the timber and wood mass each one contains. The description ought to be accompanied by the length-valuations introduced in the forest.

10. *The plan of management*, of which a sketch ought to be made at the place of employment, so that the state of the forest in case of need may serve for further direction, contains the following titles :

Manner of working the forest, under which is noted for every block how great part of forest land and quantity of wood and timber suits the one or the other of the mentioned methods of working the forest, and where so required the motives for the distribution of the forest-ground between them.

Rotation, under which title separately for each block and method of working the forest with necessary motives may be introduced, the age which, in general it is thought the forest should have before the same can be consumed ; whereto with heavy timber-thinning under the title in question ought to be given the time.

Thinning-time, during which thinning shall be done.

Consumption, which title for every block contains a calculation of what, during the whole of the twenty-year period, and during every year of the same, should be consumed, also report where and how consumption ought to be effected separately for forest adapted to tract-cutting, thinning, or low-forest culture ; and there ought therewith to be added in tabular form, equally for the two foregoing titles, a compendium, (Table No. 2,) to which is added a report for the whole block and area, and amount of wood and timber summed together.

Forest-cultivating, (with special regard to sowing and planting,) under which is noted in table form, (Table III) by block-division and sub-division, the area of the ground which during the period shall undergo complete forest-cultivating, (that is, clearing and raising forest again on the same place by planting or sowing,) help-culture, drainage or other means for advancing re-growth, whereto may be noted the nature of the measures and steps which in every case shall be adopted.

Project for the future division of the forest in respect to rotation and thinning periods, under which title, and with reference to the map of the forest, is indicated how it is considered, on the basis of the present state, the sub-divisions ought to be united for hastening, and with least sacrifice of growth, to form suitable parts of the forest, corresponding with the twenty-year periods, separate report being made for the division of the ground in every block for tract-cutting, thinning, or low-forest growing.

Pasture and autumn-mowing, under which is noted that which, with regard to the subject, should be observed during the division period.

Means of facilitating the transportation and sale of wood and timber, under which title is given, as may happen, the needful scheme for ways, improvement of floating-courses, disposing of the sorts of timber necessary for the region, &c., &c.

Administration and care wherewith representation is made of what, in said respect, ought to be adopted to secure suitability of plan of economy, therewith always complying with what is prescribed by the control-book for consumption and forest-cultivation.

11. *Rotation with tract-cutting* is determined so that, after knowledge is acquired of the kinds of trees the forest will yield, and the growing-time required for them, the area of the forest-grown land is divided into the number of twenty-year periods which said growing-time contains ; thus, with 140 years growing-time by 7, with 120 years by 6, &c.,

whereby is ascertained the extent on an average can be consumed during every 20 years. Thereafter is examined through comparing the extent of this latter with the area which every age-class takes up, how long time consumption in each and every class, beginning with the oldest, should require, wherewith also knowledge is gained of the age of the forest at the time of consumption. If then it is found that any essential part of the forest should be consumed first after that which has taken injury from too high age, so ought said examination to be renewed in a twenty years' shorter time, and in proportion to the therewith greater area of consumption, till its results shows that the forest can be consumed without losing in value, when the last-mentioned time is adopted for rotation-time.

With the introduction of regulated timber-thinning it is seen, too, that the thinning-time becomes so sufficient that a requisite number of trees may be able to grow to heavy timber by the time its thinning returns to the same tract which it before went over.

As well rotation as thinning-time should contain a certain number of twenty-year periods.

Thinning-time ought to be an equal part of rotation time.

12 The computation of what is taken out by tract-cutting during the period is made thus:

Of that part of the forest-grown land allotted to tract-cutting is assigned for *consumption* during forty years, two-sevenths of the area with one hundred and forty year, two-sixths or one-third with one hundred and twenty year, two-fifths with one hundred year rotation periods, &c. Out of the oldest age-classes is taken off thereafter as great area as corresponds to said part. The forest which is found on the area thus taken off consists of that which can be consumed during forty years. Hereof is allotted for consumption during the first twenty years, out of the oldest or least growing bestand, so great a part that the growing forest thereon, *without* including the grown, may attain to wood and timber mass equally with the growing forest on the other part, *with* reckoning or including that grown during twenty years. With the reckoning of growth, nevertheless, so-called growth-tables may not be used unless the yearly growth of the bestand running in the two periods is accepted as the average amount of what these during its filled age yearly grow.

In thinning of heavy timber is consumed, during the time adopted for thinning, all the timber found at the dividing or allotment besides half the quantity of heavy timber-stuff which within the period of thinning can grow. Of this amount of wood and timber can thus be consumed during the twenty-year division period, with forty-year thinning-time half, with sixty-year one-third, and with eighty-year one-fourth. In this way is taken off that part of the forest which shall correspond with the first twenty-year period, wherewith is observed, nevertheless, that only such land as bears heavy timber, or within the thinning period grows heavy or merchantable timber-stuff, enters into the calculation, also that the part taken off does not more than twenty-five per cent. exceed that which the land just mentioned, reckoned exclusively according to the area, shall have produced in the period. If it is found, notwithstanding such augmentation in area, the part taken or sold off does not contain the number of pieces of timber which, according to the above-mentioned calculation, ought to be had, the consumption is reduced to what the thus sold-off district for a period of twenty years can according to calculation give.

With other thinning the consumption's mass is calculated the same as is mentioned in regard to track-cutting.

In the dividing or allotment for low-forest growing, with separate blocks the area is divided by that number of periods which the rotation-time contains, after which the amount of consumption is fixed according to the bulk of production on that part which corresponds to the first period, wherewith, if so required, the growth is reckoned in the manner above written.

In the consumption calculated in harmony with the above principles is not included what, according to estimate, is obtained through preparatory thinning and help-pruning or clearing up of found wind-falls and dry forest, so called cleaning-cutting, likewise neither the utilizing of stumps, roots, branches, and twigs.

13. When the division or allotment takes place in such forests as are mentioned in Chapters III and V of the Government's Forest Regulations of 29th June, 1866, with the dividing proceedings and maps shall special memorial be prepared, representing how far it is thought the forest, according to §§ 16 and 23 of said regulations, ought to be placed under the immediate care and administration of the forest state, also if such is not the condition, the need of the products of the forest at the homestead or farm to which it belongs; also how far the forest is insufficient to supply said need, or nevertheless besides answering the requirement or leaving something over the same, and in the latter case the amount of surplus, also project for the forest-rent, which according to § 17 ought to be reckoned, or that portion of clear gain which, on the principle of § 24 of regulations, can accrue to the resident occupier.

14. At the *revision* of the allotment which here above is ordained is drawn up on the prin-

ciple of examination of the forest, and, with high-forest culture, accurate calculation of the older age-classes, new allotment proceedings, wherewith the map is intended for introducing of the noticed changes.

Revision shall also be had of the forest-maps and plans of economy hitherto drawn up for the public forests, where these have been operative twenty years or more. Should the maps and allotment proceedings be found continuing suitable the drawing up of new ones may be dispensed with.

Stockholm, as above.

A. E. ROS.

C. A. T. BJÖRKMAN.

[Translated from the Swedish.]

5. His Royal Majesty's gracious regulations concerning the management of the public forests within the Kingdom. Given at the Palace of Stockholm, June 29, 1866.

We, Charles, with the grace of God, the King of Sweden, Norway, &c., &c., make known that, whereas the estates of the Kingdom in their humble letters of February 16, 1858, and November 30, 1863, have made known the principles according to which the public forests of the Kingdom ought to be managed, we have found proper, having heard the opinion of our forest administration, and of ours and the Kingdom's Exchequer College, (Kammar Kollegium,) and canceling the royal regulation for the forests within the Kingdom of August 1, 1805, in regard to land and commons, Crown-parks, and forests belonging to the Crown, as well as to forests belonging to dwelling-places and farms of the Crown, and, furthermore, altering other regulations in regard to the same subject, as far as contrary to these rules, in accordance with the principles adopted by the estates of the Kingdom, to stipulate the following:

CHAPTER I.

IN REGARD TO CROWN-PARKS.

§ 1. The crown-parks shall be retained to their original extent, and managed according to such plans which, based upon scientific rules and suited to different locations, shall promote the conservation and the yield of the forests. Our forest administration shall sanction the plans of management and issue such orders as may be necessary for the proper care of these forests.

§ 2. The crown-parks shall be under the immediate care and management of the forest corps. The Crown shall defray the expenses for their guarding, and shall alone receive the income of the same, where not otherwise is stipulated.

§ 3. Regulations issued in regard to crown-parks shall also be in force in regard to quicksand fields belonging to the Crown.

§ 4. In regard to the Royal Deer Park at Stockholm, as well as commons belonging to the Crown and assigned to certain purposes, public establishments or institutions are separately stipulated.

CHAPTER II.

IN REGARD TO COMMONS.

§ 5. What is stipulated in § 1 in regard to crown-parks is also valid in regard to commons.

§ 6. Part owners of commons will build and live within the district according to their part, where not in separate cases otherwise is stipulated. Our governor of province shall annually fix and publish time and place when these part owners shall, by proxy from the parish and by balloting, select an administration, which, in all cases concerning the common, shall exercise the decisive right of the part owners, when not otherwise is stipulated in the rules for the common. These rules are made out by the part owners and sanctioned by our governor of province as far as he shall find the the same, having heard the opinion of the district manager, corresponding to the laws and these regulations, as well as to the adopted plan of the management of the commons.

§ 7. If the part owners wish themselves to guard and manage the common they may do so under condition—

1. That a plan of the management of the common has been approved of by our forest administration and that the preparing works necessary for the surveys are made at the expense of the part owners; and

2. That regulations are issued and sanctioned for the common as mentioned in the foregoing section.

§ 8. If the part owners guard and manage the commons the respective forest officers shall, however, observe that what is prescribed for the management of the forest is properly observed. Should there be any neglect herein, and should the same not be corrected within the time specified by our governor of province, or should larger felling be done on the common than permitted in the plan of the management, our governor of province shall order the common to be placed under the care or management of the forest corps; whereafter the forest administration, report hereof having been made, shall appoint the respective manager of the "rivier" to take care of the guarding and management of the common through foresters engaged for the purpose.

§ 9. Should not the part owners guard and manage the common, this shall be done by the forest corps in the manner above mentioned.

§ 10. Of the yield of the common shall in the first place be paid out the salary of the foresters, the cost of the maintenance of their dwelling-places, forest cultivation, felling of forest products which are not growing, as well as other expenses mentioned in the plan of management or especially ordered.

§ 11. Thereafter shall the timber required for bridges and other buildings within the district be laid aside, and the remainder of the yield be annually divided between the part owners, depending upon the decision of the part owners whether the products or the returns for the same shall be divided between them. Should the common be under the care and management of the forest corps, the yield, whether in products or money, shall be placed at the disposal of the administration of the common, who shall pay out and divide the same according to above-mentioned principles.

§ 12. Should the common be managed by the forest corps "it shall be the duty of the "rivier" manager to annually, before the end of the month of July, render account for the past calendar year of not only the yield of the common in forest products, but also of the expenses for the common and of the funds he has received for the covering of the same. This account shall be made out in two copies, of which one is to be transmitted to our forest administration and the other to our governor of province. It shall be the duty of the common administration to transmit to our governor of province, before the end of the month of August, annual accounts of the yield of the commons and of the distribution of the same among the part owners, or how otherwise disposed of. Should the common be under the care and management of the part owners, this account shall also embrace a list of the felling as well as of the expenses of the common during the past account year, and will in such a case be transmitted to our governor of province to the forest administration after the lapse of the thirty days mentioned in the following section.

§ 13. The accounts mentioned in the foregoing section having been received by our governor of province, they shall be open for examination by the part owners at the meeting mentioned in section six and during thirty days at the time and place fixed and published by our governor of province.

§ 14. Former instructions for a common respectively sanctioned may be in force, provided they correspond with these rules. Should an alteration be necessary, such may be done according to what is stipulated in section six for the issuing of new regulations.

CHAPTER III.

IN REGARD TO THE FORESTS BELONGING TO THE KING'S DOMAINS OR LET-OUT FARMS AND ESTATES OF THE CROWN.

§ 15. At the King's domains, the King's dairies, dwelling-places assigned to the finances of the States, (Statsverket,) and other farms and estates which are managed or let out for the account of the Crown, shall a regular forest management be introduced, provided they are not situated within the same territory as any private property; or, should there be any other objection, they shall be surveyed where our forest administration, with regard to the extent and quality of the forest, shall find it suitable. The cost of the survey shall be paid out of public funds, where not in existing leases otherwise is provided.

§ 16. Should the forest be very large and so located that the same may conveniently be placed under the immediate care and management of the forest corps, we will, upon the report of our forest administration, in each separate case, issue regulations therefor, and in such cases it shall be observed that sufficient forest is retained for household purposes, but the remaining forest, as now existing leases expire or the lessee will consent, shall be made into a crown-park, and managed according to Chapter I.

§ 17. In all the leases issued hereafter for the estates of the Crown, the lessee shall engage himself to care and manage the forest according to the plan of management where such has been or shall be sanctioned with the right to freely dispose of that yield of the forest even above what is required for household purposes; and when plans of management are made out for such forests as will remain under the care and management of the lessee, a certain amount of forest rent shall be fixed therefor and mentioned among the conditions of the lease. It shall depend upon the opinion of our and the Kingdom's Exchequer College, (Kammar Kollegium,) or the authority under the care and superintendence of which the estate is placed, whether, and under what conditions, the above right to dispose of the forest may be granted the present lessee for the remaining time of the lease.

§ 18. When forests belonging to the estates of the Crown are placed under the management of the lessee, it shall be the duty of the respective foresters to carefully watch over that the plan of management is followed and to report all neglects of the same.

CHAPTER IV.

IN REGARD TO FORESTS BELONGING TO THE FARMS OF PUBLIC INSTITUTIONS.

§ 19. In regard to forests belonging to the farms and estates of churches, academies, hospitals, soldiers' asylums, and other public institutions, what is stipulated in Mom. 1, § 15, about district felling and other regular management, shall be in force, and the respective administration or authority who shall have the superintendence over such property ought to apply to our forest administration to obtain the plan of management, who shall order the respective forester to make out such a plan and to transmit the same to the forest administration for approval, for which service he will be separately paid in accordance with the tariff.

§ 20. The plan of management for such a forest having been approved of, it shall be the duty of the respective forester to see to that the same is observed and to report to our forest administration all neglects herein, and also, when the farm is managed by lessee or owner, to the administration or authority who superintends the same.

§ 21. In regard to farms belonging to public institutions, and which are cultivated by right of possession, is stipulated in the fourth chapter.

CHAPTER V.

FOREST BELONGING TO OFFICIAL DWELLING-PLACES.

§ 22. What is prescribed in Mom. 1, § 15, about district felling and other regular management shall be valid in regard to forests belonging to dwelling-places assigned to civil, military, and clerical institutions. Where such forests have not been surveyed as far as funds assigned for the purpose will allow, or when the possessors or administrations will defray the expenses for the same, the most suitable plan of management shall be adopted and our forest administration shall appoint a respective forester who, being separately paid for his service according to the tariff, shall survey and make out the plan of management to be transmitted to our approval by our forest administration. In making out such a plan, it shall be taken into consideration that the annual requirements of the owner of forest and pasture are filled as far as possible, even if the increase of the yield of the forest should be delayed.

§ 23. Should the forest belonging to a dwelling-place be very much larger than is required for household purposes, we will, upon the proposition of our forest administration, order the entire forest or a proper part thereof to be placed under the immediate care and management of the forest corps, as stipulated in regard to crown-parks; otherwise it shall be the duty of the farmer to guard and manage the forest, thereby observing the plan of management approved of by the forest administration.

§ 24. Until such a regulated management as mentioned in § 15 has been introduced in forests belonging to dwelling-places the owner may use the same for household purposes, when not a more extensive right has been granted him during his time of service; but thereafter may the owner, besides that he always shall enjoy that much of the income of the forest which is due to him through his previous right and what is necessary for the household purposes, if the forest is placed under his own care, receive a certain amount of the yield, which amount may, according to the greater or smaller expenses for the care of the forest, be fixed up to half the amount of the yield above what is required for household purposes. In regard to how much of the yield of the forest shall be the owner's, a regular management having been introduced, our forest administration shall, before the plan of management is approved, transmit to us their humble proposition, whereupon we, having learned the opinion of the respective parties, will decide separately in each case.

Out of the returns from forests belonging to dwelling-places shall first and foremost the expenses for its care be covered; but money advanced for the survey only be paid back in the proportion the dweller shall receive all he requires for household purposes.

The returns of the yield of forests belonging to dwelling-places which do not go to the dweller shall be disposed of at military dwelling-places by the direction for the same. At clerical dwelling-places it shall be used in conformity with the royal regulation of July 11, 1862, to regulate the income of the clergy; and shall, at the dwelling-places for the governor of province, go to the funds for regulating the salaries of the governor of province, but in all other cases to the forest-planting funds.

§ 25. What is stipulated in the foregoing section concerning the disposal of the returns of forests belonging to dwelling-places shall be in force with regard to the compensation the dweller will receive when oak-trees are felled on the farm for the account of the Crown.

§ 26. When the parishioners shall build or repair the church or the house of the parson, they may take the necessary timber from the forest of the parsonage or other farms belonging to the same, as far as survey may be held, according to the approved plan of management, without infringement upon the right of the owner to the returns of the forest.

§ 27. When forest belonging to a dwelling-place, according to § 23, is managed by the forest corps, the manager of the "rivier" shall account for the same, in the manner prescribed for commons in § 12, Mom. 1; and our governor of province shall, after the dweller has seen of the account, transmit the same, and the surplus money for military dwelling-places, to the direction for the same, and for the clerical ones to the respective domkapitlet, (cathedral chapter,) which authorities shall, when requested, hand over to the dwellers their respective shares.

In regard to the account of other forests belonging to dwelling-places, the authority who superintends the same will issue necessary instructions.

§ 28. What is stipulated in § 17 shall be in force in regard to military dwelling-places let out for the account of the salary-fund.

CHAPTER VI.

IN REGARD TO FORESTS BELONGING TO PUBLIC FARMS CULTIVATED BY TENANTS.

§ 29. The forest belonging to farms owned by the Crown and public institution may be used for household purposes, provided not otherwise stipulated by special permission or prescriptions. However, in regard to crown-farms, our governor of province, and, in regard to other farms, the authorities under whose care they are placed, may, upon application, permit the owners to use the forest, even for sale, if they only observe the plan of management approved for the same.

§ 30. If such a special permission as mentioned in section 29 is granted, the owner shall apply to our forest administration for the plan of management. The forest administration will then appoint a forest officer, who is paid by the owner according to the tariff, to make out a plan of management, which is transmitted to the forest administration for approval. It shall be the duty of the officers of the forest corps, as well as of the foresters, to see to that the plan of management is observed, and to report to our governor of province, or the authority who superintends the farm, any transgression or neglect of the same; and if such is the case in regard to crown-farms, our governor of province shall, if necessary, and until otherwise decided, prohibit the use of the forest for other than household purposes.

§ 31. In regard to the right of tenants of crown-farms, settlers and owners of settlements in the six northern læns of using the forest over and above what is required for household purposes, is separately stipulated.

CHAPTER VII.

IN REGARD TO ADVANCES FROM PUBLIC FUNDS FOR FOREST SURVEYS.

§ 32. There, upon humble proposition, we have found proper that the expense of the survey of such public forests which are not at ours and the Crown's immediate disposal may be paid by advances from public funds, there shall the advances be paid back from the yield of the surveyed forest; and for this purpose shall, in the first place, the returns from the sale of the timber which has been followed on the lines of survey be used; if these means should not be sufficient, the balance will be gradually paid in out of the annual income from the forest above what is required for the care of the forest, and in regard to dwelling-places what the dweller needs for his household purposes.

CHAPTER VIII.

IN REGARD TO PASTURE AND HAY-HARVEST IN PUBLIC FORESTS.

§ 33. Pasturing and hay-harvesting may not take place in forests mentioned in these regulations, and for which plans of management are sanctioned, in any other way than prescribed in the plan of management, or in special cases permitted by the forest administration; pasture or hay-harvest in crown-parks may be purchased for a certain time at public auctions; of pasture which may be let out on commons, the administration of the same will dispose.

3 F C

§ 34. If certain farms or communities have acquired right to pasture or harvesting in public forests, either by special resolutions or agreements, or if they have enjoyed the same as far as can be recollected, they will continue to do so until otherwise may be legally stipulated.

CHAPTER IX.

IN REGARD TO THE MARKING AND SALE OF FOREST PRODUCTS.

§ 35. In all the forests mentioned in the regulations shall trees holding at the root five decimal inches or more in diameter be worked in the prescribed order by the respective "rivier" manager or forester before they may be felled; and it shall be the duty of the party requesting the marking, or of the purchaser, to observe the rules which are prescribed by the respective foresters in regard to the felling and carrying away of such trees as well as of forest products which are not subject to marking. What is hereby stipulated shall not exist in regard to felling done in the prescribed order for household purposes.

§ 36. All sales of products from forests which are under the immediate care and management of the forest corps and from commons and dwelling-places shall be made at public auction, according to what is now or may in the future be stipulated. Time and place of auction, as well as conditions of sale, will be published by our governor of province.

§ 37. In regard to the marking and sale of forest product from crown-parks, surplus land and unsurveyed forests in the six northern læns is separately stipulated.

CHAPTER X.

GENERAL REGULATIONS.

§ 38. At examinations or surveys upon which the right of private parties is depending, the surveyor shall, after the plan of management has been made out by him, acquaint the parties whose right is in question of the plan, and they shall, within thirty days from being acquainted of the same, render their remarks to the surveyor, who shall transmit the same, accompanied by his report, to our forest administration, in case it should not be what is properly called forest land, when the remarks, with the report of the surveyor, shall be transmitted to our governor of province, whose decisions shall be submitted to the exchequer college, (Kammar Kollegium,) or any other corresponding authority, under whose jurisdiction the farm or the estate is placed.

§ 39. Should the owner of a farm, or a place mentioned in the third, fourth, and fifth chapters, wish to cultivate the forest ground belonging to the same, build a cottage, or make a pasture-ground arable, he shall apply to our governor of province, who will decide the case, after he has learned the opinion of the respective forest officer, and submit his decision to the exchequer college, or any other authority under the management of which the farm is placed. No such permission ought to be given, should the same interfere with the approved plan of management, before the forest administration has had the opportunity to give its opinion in the matter.

§ 40. Should the owner, tenant, or lessee of a public farm or place transgress the right of using the forest, afforded him by these regulations and the approved plan of management, he will be punished as far as lawful felling of forest, according to the twenty-fourth chapter of the penal laws.

§ 41. If the owner or lessee of a dwelling-place, royal farm, or other manors mentioned in the third chapter, shall neglect to do such necessary works for the care of the forest as are prescribed in the approved plan of management, and continues not to mind the same, our governor of province will order the work to be done through the forest corps, and at the expense of the neglectful party.

§ 42. The officers and attendants of the forest corps, as well as the forester, shall have the same right to report such neglects as mentioned in § 40, and to seize unlawfully felled limbs. Such timber will be sold at auctions, and the seizer will receive 20 per cent. of the net returns of the sale. The remainder shall be delivered to the institute to which the farm belongs, if the unlawful felling had been done on farms as mentioned in Chapter IV, but otherwise to the forest-planting funds, except if the unlawful felling has been done in forests belonging to farms assigned to the army, clergy, or the governors of provinces, when the stipulations in § 24 about the disposal of the share of the returns of the forest which do not belong to the owner shall be in force in regard to the above-mentioned surplus money. When a seizure is made the seizer shall immediately report the case to our forest administration, as well as to our respective governor of province; as for military farms to the respective chief of the regiment or corps. Neglect of these regulations, in regard to forests belonging to clerical farms, shall be reported by the respective parishioners.

§ 43. Should any one be dissatisfied with the decision of our forest administration concerning the management of the public forest, he may appeal to our department of finance, but not later than before 12 o'clock on the sixtieth day after he was acquainted of the decision.

§ 44. These regulations shall be in force from the 1st of July, 1867.

Which all whom it may concern shall have to obey.

In witness whereof, we have hereunto set our hand and caused our royal seal to be affixed.

The Palace of Stockholm the 29th June, 1866.

CARL. [L. S.]

J. A. GRIPENSTEDT.

[Translation from the Swedish.]

6. *His Royal Majesty's gracious regulations concerning the survey and sale of products of the forests in the læns (counties) of Stora Kopparberg and Norrland, belonging to the Crown. Given at the palace of Stockholm, December 21, 1865.*

We, Charles, with the grace of God the King of Sweden, Norway, &c., make known that, whereas the estates of the kingdom have requested us, in gracious letter of the 2-th of October, 1860, to take into gracious consideration whether or not the principles stipulated in gracious letters of April 11, 1841, and November 24, 1857, for the surveys of the forests of the crown-lands in the læns of Westerbotten and Norrbotten, also ought to be in force for the læns of Wester-Norrland, Jemtland, Gefleborg, and Stora Kopparberg, and, furthermore, in gracious letter of November 30, 1863, have proposed that, in regard to the right of using the forest over and above what is required for household purposes, which tenants of crown-lands, settlers, and owners of settlements in the six northern læns ought to have, they should be maintained in the more extensive privileges which they, compared to other tenants, hitherto have enjoyed, but under that control which, for preventing of misusage, might be prescribed; thus we have, having heard the opinion of our forest administration and of ours and the kingdom's exchequer college, (Kammar Kollegium,) found proper to cancel our above-named gracious letter and all that is stipulated in regard to the survey of the above-named læns, and to sanction the following:

§ 1. All felling of forest, except for household purposes, as mentioned in § 6, on the territories of crown-lands, or settlements on crown-parks, surplus land, unsurveyed forests, and on the land for which the saw-mills pay forest rent in the læns of Stora Kopparberg and the six læns of Norrland, shall in the future be done first after they have been surveyed by a respective forest officer.

§ 2. The following will have exclusive right of marking trees for felling:

1. Owners of crown-lands and settlements, in regard to the territories which have been allotted to them by the surveyor or provisionally marked during the survey:

2. Owners of tax-paying and freehold estate in regard to the territories provisionally marked out;

3. Owners of crown-land and settlements, as well as owners of tax-paying and freehold estate, whose land is surveyed or provisionally marked out, in regard to a certain tract of crown-land, which generally, or where local circumstances do not require an exception, is calculated for single farms or settlements, a distance of one-eighth of a Swedish mile in all directions from the dwelling; for smaller villages of not more than three families, a distance of one-quarter of a mile, and for larger villages one-third of a mile; it shall thereby be observed that, if farms or settlements which do not together make a village are situated so near each other that certain ground should, according to the above-mentioned principles, belong to them all, they shall have the same right to survey; and

4. Owners of saw-mills in regard to the land assigned to them as compensation for the privileges of felling, whether it is divided into farms or paying tax or forest rent.

§ 3. Unsurveyed dwelling-places shall also have exclusive right to survey according to the foregoing section; but in regard to the right of disposing of the marked timber, shall the regulations issued in this regard for similar dwelling-places be in force.

§ 4. For timber marked according to § 2, no stub-money or corresponding duty shall be paid to the Crown; but the one who requests the making shall have to pay the cost of the same, according to the rules His Royal Majesty may prescribe.

§ 5. Application for marking according to § 2 shall be made to the respective forest officer before the 1st of March the same year the marking is desired. The forest-officer shall thereafter, before the 1st of October of the same year, examine and mark the trees in the presence of the applicant, all in accordance with §§ 9 and 10. Beams and saw-timber which may be felled during the year shall be provided with the crown-mark. In regard to other kinds of timber, marking may be done for as many as five years at the same time, and in such a case it shall be decided how much and what kind of timber may be annually felled on each part of the forest. Before the surveyor leaves the place he shall give the applicant, free of charges, a record of the survey, for which he shall obtain a receipt. The cost of the survey shall be entered in the record. Should the applicant be dissatisfied with the survey mentioned in this section, he may appeal to our forest administration before 12 o'clock on the sixtieth day from the time the surveying documents were handed to him.

§ 6. Felling may also be done within the territories mentioned in § 2, as far as needed, for the household purposes of the farms, settlements, or dwelling-places.

§ 7. The timber from crown-parks, surplus land, and that part of unsurveyed forest to which no one has the exclusive right of felling according to § 2, shall be sold to the highest bidder.

§ 8. For the purpose mentioned in the foregoing section the respective district directors shall annually make out a felling project for each crown-park or other forest-land within their "rivier," according to the approved plan of survey and management, and to the knowledge of the quantity of timber of other crown-lands mentioned in the foregoing section, and transmit the same to our governor of province before the 1st of April. Should private parties, companies, or communities wish to have their land surveyed, they shall apply, in writing, to the respective district director before the 1st of March the same year the survey is desired, and he shall, provided there be no reasonable objection, make out a felling project for the same. Should he not be sufficiently acquainted with the tract, he shall make a preliminary survey of the same at the expense of the applicant.

§ 9. The felling ought to be so done as not to ruin the forest, and that always the same number of trees, suitable for timber and deal, may be got every year. Full-grown forest ought not to be spared so long as to be unfit for use by being too old. In regard to this our forest administration shall give the respective district directors necessary orders. At the survey of forest-land which has been on fire the trees damaged by the same ought to be first felled.

§ 10. The following kind of trees may be marked for felling:

1. Mast and large timber trees.
2. Trees suitable for beams and saw-timber, and which are 9 inches in diameter at the height of 24 feet from the root.
3. Crooked and short trees, which never can be suitable for beams or saw-timber of the above-named size.
4. Leaved, wind-fallen, and damaged trees, as wells as stubs and roots, which may be used for making charcoal, tar, or potash.

For account of privileged saw-mills, having territories assigned to them, may trees of a diameter of 5½ decimal inches at the top end be marked for felling.

§ 11. In regard to the value and fitness for different purposes of the trees intended for sale, they shall be thus classified in the plans for felling:

1. Mast and large timber-trees.
2. Growing trees for beams.
3. Growing trees for larger saw-timber.
4. Growing trees for smaller saw-timber.
5. Trees having been on fire or otherwise slightly damaged, suitable for beams.
6. Trees having been on fire or otherwise slightly damaged, suitable for larger saw-timber.
7. Trees having been on fire or otherwise slightly damaged, suitable for smaller saw-timber.
8. More damaged and wind-fallen trees for beams.
9. More damaged and wind-fallen trees for larger saw-timber.
10. More damaged and wind-fallen trees for smaller saw-timber.
11. Loads of timber for manufacturing purposes.
12. Loads of forest products for making charcoal, tar, or potash.

Trees being, 24 feet from the root, 14 decimal inches in diameter are considered suitable for beams.

Trees being, at the same height, 9 to 14 decimal inches in diameter are suitable for large saw-timber, and those having a diameter of 5½ decimal inches at the height of 16 feet for smaller saw-timber.

One load of timber for manufacturing purposes is equal to one-third of a "famn," or Swedish cord of wood of 114 cubic feet, outside measure.

§ 12. In making out plans for felling, the surveyor shall divide the territories to be surveyed in certain felling districts according to the locality and quality of the forest, and, besides, propose the way by which the timber may be most conveniently transported.

§ 13. It shall be the duty of our governors of provinces to arrange the auction-sale of the timber as soon as in receipt of the plans and guided by the proposition of the district director, transmitted to them, to stipulate the conditions of sale at the auction, however, without fixing a lowest price. Our governors of provinces shall especially see to that a suitable part of the timber felled within each district is offered for sale in smaller lots of 50 beams and 100 saw-timber or loads.

§ 14. Should the felling project embrace a tract where the owner of saw-mill is entitled to fell trees, he shall be made acquainted with the same through the care of our governor of province before the auction is published, and the owner shall within a certain specified time inform within which tract he prefers to get the number of trees or saw-timber to which he is entitled by the privileges of the mill; and this ought to be separated from what is going to be sold and assigned to the mill against the payment of the fixed stub-money.

§15. It shall be the duty of our governors of provinces to have marking-lists made out immediately after the auction and in accordance with the project for felling and the records of the auction; according to these lists the respective officers execute the marking. Our governors of provinces shall manage so that the lists are delivered to the district directors if possible before the 1st of June.

§ 16. The district officer shall mark the sold timber according to the lists, thereby observing that when several persons have purchased timber within the same tract the latter are as equally favored as possible in regard to the facilities of transporting the timber. All trees intended for beams and saw-timber shall be provided with the crown-mark, and the district officer ought to mark out the different tracts assigned to the different purchasers. Our forest administration shall besides give the foresters all the detailed instructions necessary for the marking and the felling of trees.

§ 17. Each survey shall embrace crown-parks and other territories for which a separate project has been made out. At least fourteen days before each survey the same shall be published from the pulpit of the parish church and the time named when the surveyor may be expected to each separate tract. The next Sunday after a survey, it shall also be published from the pulpit that the same is finished. Should any one consider the surveyor having infringed upon his right according to § 2, or unjustly distributed the timber between the respective purchasers within the same tract, he may appeal to our governor of province not later than 12 o'clock on the fifteenth day after the last-named publication, in consequence whereof no felling of the marked timber shall take place until the above-mentioned fifteen days have elapsed. All surveys ought to be finished if possible before the 1st of October every year.

§ 18. Marked timber ought to be felled and carried away from the forests of the Crown before the 1st of June the year next after the survey; however, our governor of province shall, when fixing the condition of the auction-sales, or upon special application, and after having heard the opinion of the respective foresters, grant a longer time for this purpose, but not more than five years from the time of the survey, of which fact the respective foresters ought to be informed. Should the purchaser neglect his duties in regard to the above, he shall forfeit his right to the timber.

§ 19. Should our forest administration find that a crown-park for which the plan of survey and management is made out may during a longer period of years yield a larger number of beam and timber trees, the right to fell a certain number of trees after the annual marking has been done may be offered for sale, the right to continue during a term of twenty years; and our forest administration shall make a contract with the purchaser to be submitted to our own gracious judgment. Such a contract may not prevent the usual marking of other timber than those specially mentioned above.

§ 20. When felling and carrying away of marked timber are done, the workmen ought to be provided with the marking-list, record of auction, or a special certificate of permission of our governor of province to show the Crown and forest officers, whenever requested; otherwise risking, to be ordered to discontinue their work.

Which all whom it may concern shall have to obey.

In witness whereof we have hereunto set our hand and caused our royal seal to be affixed.

The Palace of Stockholm, December 21, 1865.

CARL. [L. S.]

J. A. GRIPENSTEDT.

His Royal Majesty's gracious regulations in regard to the establishing of crown-parks in the læns of Stora Kopparberg and Norrland, and to certain rules to be observed at the separation of common grounds into distinct possessions (storskiften) and settlements in the above-mentioned læns. Given at the palace of Stockholm, December 21, 1865.

We, Charles, with the grace of God the King of Sweden, Norway, &c., make known that, whereas the states of the Kingdom at the Riksdag humbly represented the necessity of retaining suitable tracts of the crown-lands within the læns of Stora Kopparberg and Norrland as crown-parks, thus we have found proper graciously to stipulate the following:

§ 1. Already existing surplus land of the Crown, as well as they which arise from present divisions and "storskiften," shall, where such is suitable, on account of their being situated together, of the general quality of the forest ground and of the forest itself, facilities of floatage, sale of forest products, demand for timber in the locality, and other similar circumstances, be retained and managed as crown-parks.

§ 2. In order to ascertain the above-mentioned circumstances our governor of province in the læns of Stora Kopparberg, Gelleborg, Wester-Norrland, Jemtland, Westerbotten, and Norbotten, shall, where such is not already done, have the place examined by a specially-appointed surveyor and officer of the forest corps, and humbly report to us upon the subject; whereafter we will graciously order which of these grounds shall be placed under the care and management of the forest corps. Has such a farm or settlement arisen from a previous survey, it shall be separated again from the crown-park.

§ 3. When survey or "storskiften" is hereafter done in any parish, there shall also certain ground be assigned to one or several crown-parks, provided such is necessary and there is suitable locality. At the survey shall, therefore, not only the ground which is particularly suitable for cultivation be assigned to new settlements and older settlements and farms, but it shall also be seen to that the ground which has less facilities for cultivation on account of the circumstances mentioned in § 1, and therefore suitable for crown-park, is properly separated from the property of private persons. The interest of the Crown shall, in this case, be guarded by the respective forester, and the surveyor shall, therefore, always call the former to the meetings held with the farmers for the division of the ground. Should he propose the establishing of a crown-park, the surveyor shall, after the survey and the map is finished, but before the final project to division or "storskifte" is made out and the same is executed, together with the forest-officers, make out a provisional project of places for one or several crown-parks, and submit the same to the judgment of our forest administration, who shall make the remarks they may have reason to make. The case is hereafter decided by our governor of province, together with the whole of the survey.

§ 4. From unsurveyed forest may, before the general survey is done, certain ground be assigned for crown-parks, should the forest administration find it necessary and if there is sufficient ground within the parish for already-established farms and settlements. In such cases shall our governor of province, at the request of our forest administration, separate the ground in question from neighboring farms and settlements, and shall thereby also what is stipulated in regard to the division of ground in other parts of the læns of Westerbotten and Norrbotten be in force for Lapland.

§ 5. Old farms and settlements shall in the future, as heretofore, receive at divisions and "storskiften" that space of forest and ground to which they are entitled according to regulations; but should there be question about separation into a crown-park, the forests of the farms ought to be so situated that the crown-park will receive natural boundaries of water or impediments, and be thus separated from the private properties. Should this not be possible, the farms may keep the pasture and forest sufficient for household purposes within the crown-park, but their other forest property will have to be situated outside the crown-park.

What is prescribed in this section shall also be observed when, under general survey, a certain piece of ground is assigned to saw-mills, as a compensation for the lost privilege of felling trees, in accordance with our gracious letter to ours and the kingdom's exchequer college (Kammar Kollegium) of May 29, 1852.

§ 6. The cost of the different surveys mentioned in §§ 2 and 4 shall be paid from the forest-planting funds, it depending upon the representation of the forest administration and upon our special gracious judgment whether, with regard to the surveys mentioned in § 4, some part of what has been paid by the forest-planting funds shall be returned from the funds assigned toward the general surveys.

Which all whom it may concern shall have to obey.

In witness whereof we have hereunto set our hand and caused our royal seal to be affixed.

The Palace of Stockholm, December 21, 1865.

                                                  CARL. [L. S.]

J. A. GRIPENSTEDT.

His Royal Majesty's gracious proclamation prohibiting new settlements for the present. Given at the palace of Stockholm, December 21, 1865.

We, Charles, with the grace of God the King of Sweden, Norway, &c., make known that, besides having, in consequence of the humble proposition of the estates of the kingdom when last collected, in regard to the forest management within the northern læns of the kingdom, under this day, transmitted to the estates of the kingdom now collected our gracious proposition with regard to altered regulations about the assignment to private parties of the crown-land in Norrlands and Stora Kopparberg's læn, we have, in connection therewith, found proper graciously to stipulate that our gracious letter of May 25, 1860, to ours and the kindom's exchequer college, (Kammar Kollegium,) prohibiting new settlements upon surveyed surplus land in the northern læns, shall also exist for Stora Kopparberg's læn, and that, in regard to crown-lands for which survey not yet has been sanctioned, no permission to found new settlements upon such land will be at present granted.

Which all whom it may concern shall have to obey.

In witness whereof we have hereunto set our hand and caused our royal seal to be affixed.

The Palace of Stockholm, December 21, 1865.

CARL. [L. S.]

J. A. GRIPENSTEDT.

———

[Translation from the Swedish.]

7. *His Royal Majesty's gracious regulations concerning the right to dispose of forests on such "skattehemman" (estates for which rent or tax is paid to the Crown or to a private person) as are created by settlements, which are leased from the Crown, or by such older settlements on which the prescribed conditions of building and cultivating have not been duly fulfilled. Given at the palace of Stockholm, June 29, 1866.*

We, Charles, with the grace of God the King of Sweden, Norway, &c., make known that, whereas the estates of the kingdom, in writing of the 15th instant, have announced their approval of our gracious proposition of the 21st of December, last year, concerning amended directions in regard to the lease to private persons of the land of the Crown in the læns of Norrland and Kopparberg, we have found proper, in accordance therewith, graciously to sanction the following rules:

§ 1. On "skattehemman," arising from settlements, of which hereafter the Crown may grant a lease, the owner shall have no other right to the forest of the estate than to take sufficient timber and fuel for household purposes, without survey, and after survey and marking by the Crown officers, to appropriate and sell all that, in addition hereto, may be felled without injury to the forest. Neither may, for the purpose of cultivating the soil, the forest be felled otherwise than above is indicated, unless the owner, as hereafter stated, has obtained special permission thereto from the governor of the province.

§ 2. What is prescribed in the foregoing section for estates arising from settlements on which the Crown may hereafter grant a lease shall also be in force for such estates arising from settlements on which lease already has been granted, and where the prescribed duties of building and cultivating have not been fulfilled within the time specified; and our respective governors of the provinces shall, in order to ascertain whether such is the case or not, as soon as convenient, and at least within the time when, according to existing rules heretofore, settlements ought to be inspected, order an inspection to be held, in the order prescribed, at such settlements on which the Crown has granted the lease, before the issuing of the regulations, and the accord hereof to be transmitted to our governor of the province. Should at any settlement the prescribed duties of cultivating and building not have been fulfilled within the time heretofore specified, our governor of the province shall, by a special resolution, from which appeal may be made in usual order, and where there can be no question of dispossession, declare that, since the settlement, when the duties of building and cultivating have been fulfilled at some future period, has been transferred to a copyhold estate, the owner will only have such right to the forest as is stated in § 1.

§ 3. It shall be specially stated in all the resolutions by which a settlement is transferred under the title of "skattehemman" or copyhold estate, whether the owner shall have full right to the forest belonging to the same or only enjoy the limited right mentioned in § 1; this ought to be recorded in the ground-rent book.

§ 4. For the survey and marking of such copyhold estate as mentioned in § § 1 and 2, shall our gracious regulation of December 21, 1868, concerning the marking and sale of forest products from the forests of the Crown in the læns of Stora Kopparberg and Norrland be in force. The cost of the marking shall be paid according to the principles adopted therefor by our gracious letter to the forest administration of the 11th of May of the present year.

§ 5. Should the owner of such copyhold estate, as mentioned in § § 1 and 2, wish to fell trees for the purpose of cultivation, over and above the marking for the year, he shall apply to our governor of the province, the application to be accompanied by the certificates of two creditable persons, as to the situation, extent, and quality of the ground, its fitness for cultivation, and of the time required for the completion of the same. Our governor of the province will, where further survey may be necessary, cause such a survey to be held by the respective officer, and at the expense of the applicant. Should our governor of the province find proper to grant the application, he will fix a certain time within which the applicant shall have completed the cultivation, in default of which the applicant will be suitably fined; whereupon, the forest, having been duly marked, may be felled and used by the owner as he pleases.

§ 6. Any owner of copyhold estate mentioned in § § 1 and 2 who shall infringe the right to the forest of the estate given him by this law will be punished as for unlawful felling of forest, as per the twenty-fourth chapter of the penal law. The officers of the forest corps, as well as the foresters, shall be entitled to prefer charges against such offenders, and, to seize unlawfully felled timber, the party who makes the seizure shall receive 20 per cent.; the balance shall go to the forest-planting funds.

Which all whom it may concern shall have to obey.

In witness whereof we have hereunto set our hand and caused our royal seal to be affixed.

The Palace of Stockholm, June 29, 1866.

CARL.   [L. S.]

J. A. GRIPENSTEDT.

His Royal Majesty's gracious proclamation concerning the canceling of the temporary prohibition against new settlements, of December 21, 1865. Given at the palace of Stockholm, June 29, 1866.

We, Charles, with the grace of God the King of Sweden, Norway, &c., make known that, since we, under the 21st of December last year, in connection with our gracious proposition to the States of the kingdom, concerning, among other altered regulations in regard to the lease to private individuals of the land of the Crown in the læns of Norrland and Kopparberg, by gracious order of the same day, have temporarily prohibited the granting of permission to settle upon the crown-lands, on which the felling of forest not yet has been regulated, thus, and after the States of the kingdom have announced, in writing of the 15th of this month, their consent to our proposition, and we, in consequence hereof, under this date, have issued gracious regulations concerning the right to dispose of the forests on such copyhold estates, which arise from settlements in which hereafter lease is granted by the Crown, or on such other settlements, for which the prescribed cultivation and building have not been fulfilled, therefore, we have found proper to graciously command the canceling of the above-n entioned prohibition, that on the unfelled forest of the Crown in the læns of Kopparberg and Norrland, as well as on such remaining ground in the said læns, which have, after prescribed examination, been found unfit for crown-parks, settlements may be granted to farmers, if suitable localities exist, and under condition that the rules already prescribed or graciously issued in the future may be observed.

Which all whom it may concern shall have to obey.

In witness whereof we have hereunto set our hand and caused our royal seal to be affixed.

The Palace of Stockholm, June 29, 1866.

CARL.   [L. S.]

J. A. GRIPENSTEDT.

His Royal Majesty's gracious communication to the board of domains, Kammar Collegium, June 29, 1866, concerning the disposal of such remaining land, which cannot suitably be used as crown-parks or for new settlements, &c.

Charles, &c., our grace. &c. Since we, under the 21st of December last year, proposed to the estate of the kingdom several new regulations in regard to the disposal of such surplus land or parts thereof, which are set aside by the surveys in the læns of Stora Kopparberg and Norrland, and found less suitable to be retained as crown-parks or used for new settlements, on account of their being not suitable for cultivation; and as the estates of the kingdom, in humble writing of the 15th of this month, have announced their approval of what we graciously have proposed, therefore, we have, in accordance herewith, and with regard to the opinion the honorable house of peasants has expressed concerning reindeer-pastures, and localities for which the rent is paid in butter, found proper graciously to stipulate that, with exception of what is called reindeer-pastures, the disposal of which for other purposes we do not think ought to be considered at present, such surplus land in the læns of Stora Kopparberg and Norrland which offer no inducements for cultivation, and which, either by being irregular tracts within and between the territories of villages and farms, or otherwise by its qualifications not suitable to be retained as crown-parks, shall, according to our opinion in each separate case, either where certain farms or villages use pasture-ground against butter-rent, be joined to these farms without purchase-money, but with increase of the ground-rent, in such manner as the survey regulations prescribe, or be liable to forest-rent according to the gracious regulations of June 28, 1775, and the gracious letter of December 5, 1780, about the taxation in Savolax and Karelen, and be sold with the right of ownership to the highest bidder, with duty for the purchaser, if the land is used as pasture against butter-rent, to leave the possessors undisturbed in their right to pasture and necessary fuel, as well as to timber, for such houses and fences as are necessary for the use of the pasture-ground. In both these instances, however, shall the future private owner of the land in regard to the right to use the growing wood submit to the same rules which are prescribed for owners of such farms as arise from settlements hereafter leased from the Crown, in accordance with our gracious regulations issued under this day.

And we command our governor of the lans of Stora, Kopparberg, and Narrland, when rendering their humble proposals in regard to the future disposal of surplus lands, to take into consideration if the same or parts thereof may be thus qualified as to be disposed of in either of the two above-mentioned ways.

This to all whom it may concern to obey, and we commend you to God Almighty. The Palace of Stockholm, June 29, 1866.

CARL.

J. A. GRIPENSTEDT.

His Royal Majesty's gracious letter to the board of domains (Kammar Collegium) of June 29, 1866, concerning the transferring to the forest administration the care and management of the forests within the kingdom hitherto committed to the charge of the board of domains.

Charles, &c., &c., Our Grace, &c., &c. Since our forest administration in writing, dated the 31st of last March, humbly inquired whether the time has not arrived for the transferring to them of the administration and management of the forests which hitherto has been committed to you; and you have declared in your report of the 27th following April, that the business in question and which partly, according to § 5, mom. 10, and § 8, mom. 18, of your instruction of the 16th of February, 1838, but principally, by the instruction for the forest and chase corps of the 16th of March, said year, still belonged to you, but ought, according to the above-mentioned gracious letter of the 21st of January, 1859, to be transferred to the forest administration, consisted of: 1. Examination our sanctioning of felling-districts and plan for the management of crown-parks and commons, according to § 4; 2. Similar examination of propositions in regard to the forest economy on quicksand fields, according to § 9; 3. Examination of projects for cultivating the crown-parks, according to § 31, which required the assignment of money from the forest planting funds; and 4. The taking of such measures as were prompted by the annual reports of crown-parks and commons, transmitted to you according to § 40, all in the last-named gracious instruction: and, besides, humbly stated that, in your opinion, there would be no objection to the transferring of the said business to the forest administration; thus we have issued under this day gracious regulations in regard to the economy of the common forests within the kingdom, according to which it belongs to the forest administration to examine and sanction the plans for the management of the common forests and to issue all other instructions necessary for their management in connection therewith found proper to decide, that the forest management now being your office, according to special sections of your instruction of February 16, 1838, and to the instruction for the forest and chase corps within the kingdom, of March 16, the said year, in the future shall be exercised by the forest administration, and that it consequently shall be your duty to deliver to the forest administration documents and maps belonging to the forest economy within the kingdom, now in your possession.

This to all whom it may concern to obey, and we commend you to God Almighty. The Palace of Stockholm, June 29, 1866.

CARL.

J. A. GRIPENSTEDT.

IV.—THE PROFITS OF FOREST CULTURE ON A SMALL FARM.

In a little pamphlet of 64 pages, entitled "Directions in Forest Culture for the Peasantry," by Mr. C. A. T. Björkman, secretary of the royal administration of forests, published in 1870, under the patronage of the patriotic society of Sweden, are some practical suggestions under this head, of which the following is an abstract. Mr. Björkman is also an instructor in the Royal Forest Institute, and has had upward of twenty years' practical experience in forest culture.

On one tunnland (1.22 acres) of medium fertile land closely grown with pine and spruce of from twenty to one hundred years of age, forest grows yearly to an average amount of half a famn of wood, (1 famn nearly a cord,) or 50 Swedish cubic feet. On a little forest of 50 such tunnlands the yearly growth is 25 famns. When one without damage is able yearly to consume as much as the forest during the same time grows, he thus obtains for all the future a yearly consumption of 25 famns, consisting of timber, fuel, fencing, &c., on the condition, however, that the consumption is suitably done; that no trees are here and there pulled up; also, that attention is paid to re-growth where the forest has been cut away. To such production can further be added about 5 famns obtained from branches and stumps, so that the amount rises to 30 famns. Where the consumption is thus regulated through the whole forest, the new growth of trees on the place cleared will be of larger size, and if they are close there will be an increase of fertility from the abundance of leaves, and an additional growth may be reckoned on of 10 famns; so that the whole timber-production of every sort for home need is augmented to 40 famns. On the contrary, by bad management, the growth from year to year diminishes.

The difference between regulated or economical management of a forest, and the contrary, in money valuation may be stated as follows:

10 saw-logs, at 20 cubic feet, (Swedish)	200
20 building timbers, at 15 cubic feet, (Swedish)	300
10 loads fencing, at 33⅓ cubic feet, (Swedish)	333
500 poles or stakes, at 20 cubic feet (Swedish) per 100	100
20 famns of wood	2,000
2 loads mechanical timber	67
Swedish cubic feet	3,000

or 30 famns.

With the forest economy now in use, and if the forest from the beginning was not richly seeded, it can be taken without exaggeration that timber fails after the space of twenty-five years. The purchase of such at an average price of 3.50 rix-dollars costs afterward over 100 rix-dollars a year besides hauling. After a further lapse of five years even poles are lacking, which, at 4 rix-dollars per 100, cost 25 rix-dollars. When ten years more have passed the remaining trees are all too brushy and damaged to be serviceable for fencing, which, when the same has to be bought at a price of about 3 rix-dollars a load, or 30 rix-dollars for ten loads, it will be seen a yearly outlay of over 150 rix-dollars has been laid on the farm; a burden which, when finally even mechanical timber, and for the most part fuel also, is wanted, is further increased at least 50 rix-dollars, so that the expenses for timber for domestic use amount to 200 rix-dollars; a sum which comprises the interest on 4,000 rix-dollars wherewith the value of the estate has thus been diminished, while the owner has had considerable outlay yearly in procuring domestic timber. In other words, the proper rearing and care of a forest is the creation of a permanent capital or fund the interest of which can be securely relied on.

V.—HOW A PLAN OF SYSTEMATIC FOREST ECONOMY CAN BE CARRIED OUT ON A SMALL FARM.

The so-called "tract-cutting," whereby consumption for the year is confined to a certain given clearing, usually comprising ¹⁄₅₀ or ¹⁄₁₂₀ of the forest, is undoubtedly the most desirable manner of consuming in somewhat larger forests, where annual cuttings contain all of the different sorts of timber and wood which are required for home use. But in small forests, such as are here chiefly considered, where the annual cutting cannot be expected to supply the home wants, tract-cutting must be practiced, with certain modifications, because it may happen, for example, that when one particularly needed heavy timber the annual cutting would include none other than fencing, and vice versa. This modified plan is called regulated thinning, being the same that is prescribed in the circular of the forest administration of June 20, 1867, for such lesser public forests as are not adapted to tract-cutting.

As all economy ought to be based on a plan, we will now see how one should proceed to devise without cost an inexpensive plan of regulated forest economy. Taking, for example, a forest of fifty tunnlands, (sixty acres,) one must first examine and fix in mind where the old, middle-aged, and young forest "bestands" are situated, or, if they are blended, where each of the different ages preponderate. Old forest may be designated as that one hundred years old or older, the middle-aged from forty to one hundred years old, and the young under forty years. In case it has not already been done, the forest is surveyed and marked out into three divisions, according to the three age classes, and also mapped; but if the trees are so mixed that the forest cannot be classified according to age, it should, nevertheless, be divided into three somewhat equal parts. Natural formations, hills, swamps, or the like, are to be taken in preference as boundaries of the divisions. [Here are given details as to the method of measuring the forest.] The area of the forest being ascertained, one should deduct therefrom the unproductive parts—marsh, hill or ledge—so as to know really how many acres will bear forest. Then, inasmuch as every tunnland (1½ acres) of medium forest grows as much as ½ famn, or 50 cubic feet, so it is evident that for every two tunnlands one may consume 1 famn, or 100 cubic feet, or as much as 25 famns, on an average, good forest of 50 tunnlands of actual forest land which grows young, middle-aged, and old best-ands. If the forest is thin or slow-growing, some abatement should be made, so that one calculates, for example, only 40 cubic feet on a tunnland, or, as is the same, 2 famns for every 5 tunnlands, when the yearly consumption on a forest of 50 tunnlands can amount to 20 famns. Regard should be had to the gaps or bare places, and that the annual yield of the forest is not overestimated. The principal consumption should be confined to that one of the three divisions of the forest which contains the oldest trees, and which ought to be sufficient for a third part of the rotation period, namely, forty ~ears.

How consumption shall be effected with a view to regrowth by self-seeding.—Before the consumption is undertaken one ought seasonably to estimate what timber and wood is needed for the year, so that the cutting can be well arranged, and that he shall not need to send inconsiderately at the last moment to the forest to cut. One should always seek to regulate the cutting so as to leave forests growing between the place of cutting and any naked or treeless surface. If the forest borders on an open field or lake the cutting should commence at the opposite side, so as to protect the borders of the clearing from wind and storm, and thus avoiding windfalls.

With the exception of *seed-trees* left at a distance of 6 to 8 and at the farthest 10 yards between the ends of the branches, *all* trees and bushes should be cut, inasmuch as the bushes that are left are for the most injured by bruising, and cannot become suit-able trees, and besides they produce too much shade. The branches and tops, if left, are food for forest-fires, and should be hauled away. On the other hand the finer twigs are spread over the cleared place so that the leaves during the following summer may increase the mold. In course of two or three years one finds that many pine and spruce plants have come up. In five or six years after the consumption, regrowth is usually so advanced that the seed-trees can then be cut.

After consumption in the manner stated has commenced, it is most desirable, in the cuttings which are made the following years, to extend the gap made through the first year's consumption, in doing which one proceeds in the direction from whence the heaviest winds usually come. On the other hand, one should spare the forest at the other border of the gap, which already has been somewhat tempered to the storm, and thus protects the forest lying behind. * * *

Now, if one proceeds in this manner during the forty years allotted to the first division, observing strictly not to consume more than what, according to the before-ordered calculations, he has found that the forest can bear, he will, *at the close of that period*, have consumed all the forest which at the beginning was on the first division; out in place thereof he has obtained a regrowth consisting of a new, strong, and close young forest up to the age of forty years. Meantime the second division, which was spared from all other cutting than such trimming as was needful for increasing the forest's rapid development, has grown and increased so that consumption thereof can begin, and be continued during the next forty years. At the expiration of this period consumption likewise goes over to the third division, which shall equally be sufficient during forty years; whereupon the whole forest has thus been gone through, and a new forest reared, so that ripe forest can begin to be consumed at the end of the one hundred and twenty years (rotation period) where the cutting on the first division had its beginning.

In respect to forests in the northern sections of the kingdom, where timber is cut for the market, it is to be remarked that such trees are to be selected as are ripest, wher-ever they are, leaving however about twenty to thirty seed-trees per tunnland.

How pruning should be done.—While consumption is going on as above mentioned, on the first division, the two other divisions must not be left out of view. In these divi-sions there usually occur crowded or oppressed trees, which, though approximately of the same age as the others, nevertheless have been overgrown by them. These ought to be removed, in some cases because they are dead and fallen, in others because they prevent a free development of the growing trees. This is called *help* pruning. So there are usually found in the young forest older trees, which, through their wide-extended branches, overshade it and hinder its growth, or are too old to be able to remain till the surrounding young forest is ripe. These trees ought as well to be con-sumed, which is done through the so-called *preparing* pruning or dressing. Pruning begins on the second division where it joins the first, proceeds through the third, and when that is finished begins on the new-grown forest of the first. Hereby one-twen-tieth of the forest is yearly *help-pruned*. One, however, is not obliged to prune every year if he has not need of such smaller timber and wood, but may do it every other or every third year according to need, when, of course, the extent of the tract pruned will be increased.

Till one acquires experience he must prune sparingly. Especially must pruning be sparing on light soil. * * * Pine forest is generally more pruned than spruce. Where the forest is already thin, all pruning must be postponed.

In clay-bound soil, which has the preference for spruce, the pines ought principally to be pruned off, if such are found in considerable number, and the reverse on sandy soil where pine should be the prevailing kind. Where birch occurs too plentifully in fir forests it should be pruned out and only one here and there left. * * * Next to open field or lake, from which heavy winds are apprehended, one should leave a breadth of about fifty yards unpruned. The most suitable time for *help-pruning* in young forests is early winter, when the ground is frozen but heavier snows have not yet fallen. Help-pruning yields on an average a revenue of about two famns per tunnland.

Preparatory or dressing pruning begins and continues only on the third division, and has for its object to effect an equal or harmonious forest bestand.

Cleaning-pruning is the removing of dead, injured, or sickly trees, and those scattered by windfalls, and should be done at the same time and place with the other prunings, however, before there is enough snow to greatly impede the work. If the windfalls are considerable there should be a diminution in the consumption of sound forest.

Pasture.—Generally there are rocky, unarable spots in a pasture, which should receive forest culture. For such places the white birch is recommended especially, as its leaves make good fodder, although it is not to be denied that the browsing injures the trees. The birch requires sixty years to attain its maturity.

Marshes should be drained and stocked with the gray alder, which, although it belongs to drier places, can grow on swampy tracts. Consumption can be had when the tree is twenty to thirty years old—" Handled ning i Skogs Skötsel för Allmoge," 3–66.

VI.—Explanation of certain terms in Swedish forest science.

Forest culture (skogs skötsel) includes the raising of forest, its treatment during growth, and its consumption.

By *consumption* of forest is understood the felling of trees in such a manner as to facilitate the effort of nature to produce new forest in place of the former.

Forest cultivating (skogs odling) is the raising of forest by means of sowing seed by hand, or planting.

High forest is that which is not intended to be consumed till the trees have attained their maturity.

Low forest is that which comes from shoots from the roots or stumps of former trees, and which may be consumed in a shorter time to give place to another similar crop—as, for instance, timber for hoops, hop-poles, and the like.

Rotation period. The time required, commencing with the sowing, for a forest to grow and mature.

Tract-cutting is the felling of such a portion of the forest as, according to a previously prepared plan, has been allotted for a year's supply, or such a portion as can be cut with due regard to the rotation period.

Regulated thinning is a manner of consumption, or of cutting, which is generally practised in forests where the trees in the same place are of different age.

Bestand. This word, written in Swedish " bestand," is borrowed from the German, and has a meaning in forest nomenclature for which there seems to be no corresponding English word. The original German word will therefore be adopted in this paper. The *bestand* of a forest means, in one sense, a group. There may be several *bestands* in the same forest, though the forest consists of only one sort of trees. If in a forest there is a cluster of trees of the same age, and different from its neighbors, that cluster is a *bestand.* Or if there is a body of trees of particular closeness, that body is spoken of as such a *bestand.* In short, by *bestand* is understood every part of the forest which, through variety, age, closeness or growth distinguishes it from its surroundings. The *bestand* is said to be *clean* when it consists of only one variety of trees, and *mixed*, when it comprises two or more. If these varieties are divided into groups, the *bestand* is *group-wise* mixed. The sort which occurs in greatest number is called the *prevailing*, and the others *subordinate*. With regard to age the *bestand* is called *equal* when all the trees are about equally old, and *unequal* when this is not the case. The *bestand* which contains enough trees to afford full increase is entitled *thick*, or *close* ; when the reverse, the *bestand* is more or less *thin*.

VII.—Forest science as applied in Sweden in the cultivation of the oak and certain other trees.

[What follows below in relation to growing the oak, the larch, the beech, and the pine, also as to blending forest bestands, is compiled from the Swedish work by Mr. Björkman entitled " Hand-book on Forest Culture," an octavo volume of 305 pages, illustrated, and published in 1868. Another standard Swedish work is the " Text-book on Forest Science," in two volumes, by C. L. Obbarius, published in 1845.]

1. Conditions which operate on the treatment of the oak.

And first, *soil and situation.* The oak covets a deep, mold-rich, clay soil, which should be mixed with enough sand for the free development of the roots. Of all the more common forest trees, the oak has the greatest demand of deep and good soil, and can, therefore, with as little advantage be cultivated on rocky hill tracts, with their soil, as on lean sand. Where sand is bountifully mixed with mold, the oak can indeed succeed, but it is then thought to produce less valuable timber. An exception to this rule has been noticed with respect to oaks grown on the sandy soil of the island of Oland, the timber of which is particularly strong; whereas oak timber grown on the good soil of Omberg, East Gothland, has been poor. A moist situation is serviceable for the oak; yet dry situations are preferable to wet. Southerly slopes are not favorable growing-places.

The *oak plant* is, in most respects, more hardy than the beech, yet it suffers from frost, especially as its great need of light does not permit the leaving of enough seed-trees to exclude the frost, as their shade, during the necessary time, would do more damage than frost. After it has once been oppressed, the oak plant can with difficulty be restored.

Bestand.—The strong self-pruning which takes place in the clean-oak bestand, and which, singularly, in a less fertile soil appears very early, results in a continual deterioration of the soil, while the fallen leaves, containing sharp, concentrated matter, are neither serviceable to form a good mold. After such deterioration of the forest land has continued for a considerable period the soil becomes, by degrees, all the more impotent to raise oak forest, which must finally give place to a kind of trees which are easier satisfied. This accounts for the fact that oaks are no longer found on tracts that were once famed for their oak forests. As experience has shown that the oak, less than other trees, is able to retain the land at that grade of fertility which the tree itself requires, the rule has been adopted only to raise it in company with such sorts of trees as are able to supply the needed fertility.

The oak suffers slightly from storms, because its stem extends 7 or 8 feet into the ground, and has strong side-roots to give it a firm hold. A spot in some degree protected is, nevertheless, the more preferable growing-place for the plant.

Rotation period.— Under favorable circumstances, the oak is said to attain an age of six hundred or seven hundred years. On poor and shallow soil, however, it begins to decay at middle age. On suitable spots, its age should not be less than two hundred years.

Seed-setting.—In a close bestand the oak becomes seed-bearing at eighty to one hundred, and in thinner bestands at fifty to eighty years of age, and as a free or open-growing tree, in the twentieth to the thirtieth year. On a suitable growing-place the seed-year can be reckoned on every fifth or sixth year, but on a poor soil, or in a place otherwise unfit for the tree, the interval between the fruitful years is sometimes extended to fifteen to eighteen years.

2. Consumption and means of promoting regrowth.

Clean or *naked clearing,* accompanied with sowing or planting is the most useful manner of consumption for the oak. In consequence of the plant's persistent demand for protection, light, and free situation this species is difficult to be reared without considerable help of seeding or plating. Besides, only a few oak forests are now said to be left in Sweden of a character that can be relied on for thorough self-seeding. But as the bestands of these few show that self-seeding has been possible for the oak, at least on favorable spots for growing, the method of consumption with that object will here be described.

Felling, accompanied with seed-trees.—As in consequence of the weight of the acorn a tolerably close bestand of seed-oaks must be left standing, and also as the oak bestand is oftenest thinned by self-pruning, slashing, or the felling of a number at the same time, cannot be practiced unless the consumption occurs at the seed-year. The distance apart of the branches of the seed-trees ought in general to be 10 to 15 feet, which distance, in case heavy frosts or a high growth of grass are expected, may be still further diminished if necessary; wherewith one must observe that the seed-trees bestand does not become so close as to injure the plants by overshading. Clearing to admit light is done as easily as possible, say the second winter after locating the seed-trees, or when the plants are something over a year old. Frosty situation and grass-ground unite, nevertheless, to delay *light* clearing, still it would be equally unadvisable to postpone this beyond the third winter. After the felling to admit light, by which a good part of the seed-trees are taken off, the distance between the remaining tree-branches shall be 30 to 40 feet. Final felling can be done when the plants are four or five years old, but must be postponed one or two years where the plants, in consequence of the nature of the growing-place, are in need of long-continued, gradually diminishing protection, and where thus several fellings for light are needful. That which oftenest causes delay in consumption is the state of the market for oak timber, and the greater or less demand there is for it, which circumstance may sometimes cause a delay of ten to twelve years between the placing of the seed-trees and final felling; suitable felling for admitting light occurring in the mean time in proportion as there is opportunity for selling timber.

What has been said with regard to the beech in respect to leaving a few of the finest trees here and there for still larger growth, and as to preparing the felling for receiving of the seed, and sowing or planting where regrowth is needed, applies in the main to the oak; to which may be added that satisfactory self-sowing may be counted on only exceptionally, and that a clean oak bestand should not be sought for except that the endeavor on the other hand be directed to obtaining a suitable blending with other suitable sort of trees.

3. Acorns.

The bearing-year of the oak occurs on an average every seventh year. The acorn ripens earlier or later in October, according to the weather of the previous summer. The gathering is usually undertaken that month, but may be delayed until stronger frosts occur, after which the best acorns fall from the tree. Those which fall before are for the most part prematurely ripe, or worm-eaten. Should no frost hasten their falling, the acorns may be shook off by means of a pole, at the end of which two strong pins have been fixed half a foot apart to inclose the limbs. Acorns which, notwithstanding the shaking, do not drop, are unripe, and of less value. It is not proper to beat down the acorns from the twigs, as in that case the sort just mentioned are got. To collect them in a heap, a sail-cloth or carpet is spread under the branches. Unsound and insect-injured acorns should, as far as possible, be immediately separated from them. Many old oaks often have unsound seed.

After being gathered, the acorns are spread out on the floor, in a layer not exceeding half a foot in depth, where for a week they are daily stirred. They can then be heaped to the depth of an additional foot, after which the stirring is done every other or every third day. After being thus air-dried they are moved, in case they are not to be sown during the same autumn, to a place where they are to be kept over winter. Various means have been devised for preserving acorns. The most usual, and perhaps the most secure, is to deposit them in a dry place in the neighborhood of the dwelling on a half-a-foot-thick layer of straw, in a cone-shaped pile, to the height of five feet, formed by alternate layers half a foot deep, of acorns and dry leaves or mass. The axle of the cone may be made of twigs, tied together, (and placed upright,) which serves to carry away the moisture from the interior of the cone, whose exterior may be covered with long straw to keep off the rain. Several differences prevail with regard to covering; sometimes earth is shoveled over it, and sometimes it is covered with fir twigs or with boards. That part of the twig-ventilator which extends above the cone can be capped with a coil of straw or with a suitable earthern vessel. A ditch should be dug around the cone to keep off the wet and vermin. Larger quantities can be stored in rows of cones of the same height. * * * Lesser quantities can be kept over winter in sand or saw-dust. In general acorns do not retain their growing quality longer than till the spring after they are gathered.

Sound acorns should completely fill the shell, have yellowish white unspotted kernel, and milk-white sprout or bud. A cubic foot (Swedish) of acorns weighs from 30 to 35 pounds, and numbers, when the acorns are of medium size, six thousand to seven thousand.

[It appears that acorns are not liable to injury from frost after they are ripe. The crop of acorns on the large oaks in the vicinity of Stockholm were entirely spoiled by frost before they were ripe, in the latter part of September, 1871.]

4. The sowing of acorns.

Sowing is a proceeding requiring particular attention in the cultivation of the oak, especially if it is raised in any considerable number, which, however, should only exceptionally be the case, inasmuch as timber-land in general is only in a few places and of small extent of that quality required for the oak's full development.

To render the sowing successful, the ground should be loose or deeply mellow. Acorns are usually sown in the latter part of May, so that the plants, which at first are sensitive to frost, may not come up before the spring frosts can be regarded as past. On places somewhat elevated and dry the sowing can be done in the autumn, after the acorns have been gathered and air-dried. The earth-covering varies from 1 to 2 inches, the thinner being employed on stiff soil, and the deeper on loose soil, and where the plants would be liable to appear while there was danger of frost.

Broadcast sowing.—Owing to the fact that inventions in ship-building in later times have diminished the demand for oak timber, and that broad sowing of acorns requires to be on a field about as thoroughly prepared as for grain, also that experience has furnished unmistakable proof that the clean or exclusive oak bestand is insufficient to preserve the soil in that degree of fertility requisite for such trees, broad sowing is practiced only on smaller, and especially suitable, spots, or where blended with other bestands. In the southern part of the country it is preferable to blend the oak with the beech, and in the central part with the so-called Norway spruce. The ground ought to be such that it can, without too many obstacles, like grubs and the like, be worked to the requisite depth with plow or hoe. Afterward the acorns are sown, either as grain, in which case they obtain earth-covering by harrowing, and wherein 2 cubic feet (Swedish) of acorns are required per quadrat ref, (about one-fifth of an acre,) or are laid separately in a hole made by a two-pronged hoe. * * * * In the latter case, 1 cubic foot of acorns per quadrat ref is sufficient.

Sometimes the acorns are sowed in rows; the acorns being dropped 5 to 6 inches from each other in every third or fifth furrow, according as the hand who plows progresses, in which case, the earth-covering is effected by plowing the next furrow; or, it is sometimes done by means of holes made by a board form, (with a sort of milking-stool handle placed upon it,) the taps or tenons in the form being from 4 to 5 inches long and 6 to 7 inches apart, where one large or two small acorns are dropped. In the latter process, about one cubic foot of acorns per quadrat ref are sufficient.

In row-sowing only that portion of the ground which is actually sowed is plowed, namely, belts 3 to 5 feet broad, and 5 to 8 feet apart, according as a more considerable mixture of other sorts of trees is desired. The intermediate space then receives only such preparation as the kind of tree requires, whether raised by sowing or transplanting.

Sowing in squares of one-quarter of a square foot is used most for "help culture," or when the oak is to be mixed with other sorts of trees, but can also be used in raising the oak bestand. In the latter case, the squares are hoed up to the size of at least two square feet, and at a distance from each other of 5 to 6 feet. For sowing, one cubic foot of acorns are calculated per quadrat ref. When in square sowing the earth needs to be mellowed to the depth of at least 6 inches, the process is regarded more as pit sowing, especially as earth-filling or hill-manuring is not seldom needed for the oak. A handful of such filling is required for every quadrat foot of the square's extent.

Piece sowing is on soil naturally loose, and not troubled by a strong growth of grass, and is a method of cultivating the oak, which, considering its little expense, and in comparison therewith, satisfactory results, should obtain an extensive practice. In making the hole, which should be 2 to 2½ inches deep, the "sätt"-stick, "sätt" augur, and "sätt" hammer are used. One or two acorns, according to their size, and, from previous experience, growing capacity, are dropped in each of the holes, which are at a distance of 2 to 3 feet, dependent on how little or large will be the mixture of other sorts of trees. The hole can also be made with a hoe, wherewith a strong blow is sufficient. For piece sowing, a half to two-thirds of a cubic foot of acorns are required per quadrat ref, or fifth of an acre.

5. Transplanting of the oak.

As, from what has been seen, the oak does not admit in general of being raised in separate masses or clean bestand, nor, on account of its demand for good soil, in very large connected tracts. Transplanting is a method of rearing only exceptionally used. Nevertheless it may be practiced with success where the oak is cultivated on a somewhat large scale in situations protected from frost.

The oak may be transplanted from three to four years of age up to the time it has attained a height of 15 feet. But it has been found that the setting of smaller plants and young trees of ½ to 1 inch in diameter succeeds better than the setting of medium sized five to eight year plants. These latter have, in proportion to the size of the plant, a less number of roots. Sometimes wild-growing young trees can be removed. These are, however, never so good as those reared in the plant-school, as their widely extended roots are considerably injured in taking up, which again occasions a considerable trimming of the branches; the top itself sometimes requiring to be taken off. Such rough usage, of course, injures their future growth. Plants are reared, therefore, rather in the school. For preventing a too strong development of the tap or center root, and to avoid as far as possible the cutting of the same, it has been sought to have only a shallow layer of pulverized earth in the bed of the plant when it is to be transplanted earlier than the third or fourth year of its age. It often occurs, however, that the root shoots down so deep that it must be cut off. Therefore, as this manner of incompletely preparing the ground does not accomplish the desired object, but on the contrary obstructs the natural development of the plant, it is not to be recommended.

A method of oak culture to employ in order to facilitate the transplanting and to avoid the difficulty of transferring from the fresh bed to an intermediate one, is to drop the acorns so far apart that the plants can for a longer time continue to grow at their original distance; in which case the tap-root is severed by means of a sharp spade two years before the transplanting occurs, so that the sucker roots about the cutting may be formed by the time the plants are taken up. The branches are likewise to be somewhat shortened at the same time. Although this proceeding sometimes succeeds it must nevertheless be regarded as rather hazardous where one has not the means to know immediately how much of the root has been taken off, and thereby to determine how much the branches should be clipped. On the contrary "omskolning" or the transferring of the plant from its first to an intermediate bed, should be recommended for general practice because it, in a less violent manner, prevents too great lengthening of the root and contributes more powerfully to the shooting out of small or sucker roots.

The transplanting of shoots is very expensive as well in consequence of the more troublesome taking up as the increased labor, both of digging and arranging the plant-hills, without even the setting out ; in respect to which last, if it is done with requisite care, every shoot should have a little earth-hill, which occasionally ought to be hoed or stirred up. If wild-growing shoots are used the expense is increased exceedingly through the difficulty of digging up ; in doing of which one must use specially constructed light and sharp spades in order to cut off the extended roots. The transplanting of large shoots occurs only in pasture-ground or where strong frosts are to be feared.

In other cases younger plants three to four years old are used, but only exceptionally, with clumps of earth, partly because the oak can be planted very well without, and partly because it is difficult to take up such clumps of earth of the requisite depth. As a well-pulverized earth especially contributes to the growth and success of the plants they are for the most part set in hills. If the earth has been pulverized for a year or two before, either by cultivation for root or garden crops, or by deep spading on spots intended for plants, even tenderer plants can set out, if not too bushy, with the "sätt iron " or wedge-spade.

For hill planting the young plants are not clipped at all, at least as little as possible, as the cutting necessarily injures them. If the tap-root is longer than can be set in the hill without cutting, it is better for the progress of the plant to make a hole for it in the bottom of the hill, by a pointed staff. Where filling earth is required to improve the ground it is used.

Whether larger or smaller plants are used it is important they are not set too deep. On the contrary one has nothing to fear from a shallow transplanting ; yet the earth, especially if it is hard, should be well and deeply pulverized so that even smaller, three to four years' old plants, may obtain a foot of loose earth for the outspreading of their roots.

In oak culture it is particularly material to blend the bestand in a desirable manner, and therefore to transplant other sorts of trees, which, better than the oak, contribute to the fertility of the ground between the rows of oaks. That beech and spruce are most suitable for this object has already been stated ; yet other sorts of trees can be employed. But one must observe not to select such kinds of trees that will grow so as to overshadow and crowd the oak, or at least see that these latter may obtain a suitable seed career, and that all such trees whose near standing is disadvantageous to the oak limbs are afterward cut away.

Transplanting in the spring is most suitable to the oak, but on higher situations, free from frost, it may be done in the autumn. Smaller plants obtain four feet between distance when transplanted in squares ; in rows three feet, with from 6 to 8 to 12 to 16 feet between rows, depending on the need of the soil for other sorts of trees. Larger shoots, which for the most part are set out in quadrat form, obtain a distance of 9 to 10 feet. On pasture-land the between distance is 16 to 24 feet, according as regard is had to obtaining timber or pasture. In low forests where stump plants are used with advantage these are set out at three to four years of age, at a distance of 7 to 8 feet.

6. The arch.

The larch, which in later times has been introduced into Sweden, has yet nowhere been able to come to maturity and for consumption as a bestand.   *   *

To give it a vigorous growth requires a good clay mixed and tolerably deep sand soil, and it thrives best in a moist situation. Better, however, on dry soil than wet or sour, which latter the larch cannot at all tolerate. The plant has greater need of light than the pine, and can sooner be freed from shading.

The bestand of larch should be protected from strong wind ; but it suffers less from windfalls than other species of fir trees, because of its deep roots and that its foliage falls before the heaviest storms usually occur. During the first forty to sixty years it grows rapidly, and improves the ground through its yearly falling and easy-molding leaves. After this time a strong self-pruning begins, whereby the bestand grows thin and the ground deteriorates. Like other sorts of trees which are oppressed by a strong self-pruning the larch ought not to be reared in clean bestand, but in mixture with the kinds of trees which maintain the bestand closed, so that the larch tree by this may be able, without causing any trouble to the soil, to be left to grow to higher age, when the timber first acquires a remarkable quality, namely, to withstand rotting better than most other kinds of timber. Middle-aged and young larch trees produce, on the contrary, very indifferent timber.

Rotation period.—Within its native Alp regions the larch can attain an age of six hundred years. In Sweden, and in other countries where it has been introduced, one hundred and fifty to two hundred years should be the highest age it can reach, in which case one hundred and twenty to one hundred and forty years is the most suitable period of rotation. On an unsuitable growing-place, it sometimes attains an age of only forty to fifty years.

Seed-setting.—The larch often bears seed copiously, though only a smaller part are sound. At eight to ten years of age the tree has cones, but fruitful seeds ought not to be expected at a younger age than twenty years.

7. The beech.

The soil in which the *beech* best thrives is a rich and strong loam sand, mixed clay soil, or clay-mixed sand soil, in which latter the sand should not too much predominate. Intermixture of round stones seems to be advantageous. Situation moist, but better dry than wet. The *plant* is in a high degree sensitive to frost and requires protection.

The bestand.—Among all the sorts of trees found in our forests, there is none which can be compared to the beech in respect to its quality of improving the ground. Hereto, the numerous tree-crowns, free from acid matter, contribute, as well as the easy-molding leaves. The beech is also the only one of our usual leaf-trees which, without injury to the ground, can be cultivated in clean or exclusive bestand.

Rotation-period.—On a suitable growing-place, the beech attains an age of two hundred and fifty to three hundred years. The bearing-years occur, on an average, every seven to eight years. The seed-year may be observed the autumn before, by the presence of numerous flower-buds, which are larger and plumper than leaf-buds.

8. The pine.

The *pine* occurs on soil of the most unlike quality, and in the most different situations, from the dry sand heath to the low moss where every other kind of tree is excluded. A deep and pulverized sand-soil, rich in loam and with an inconsiderable mixture of clay in moist situation, is, nevertheless, the soil whereon the pine develops the strongest growth.

The *plant* experiences no injury from frost, and only during the first two years appears to suffer from the effects of drought. Grass-growing is injurious to them, but in a less degree than to other fir-trees. As long as the bestand is closed it continues to improve the ground by its rich offal; but after the bestand becomes thin and leaves the ground without sufficient protection, the relation so changes that the pine does not prevent a gradual deterioration of the soil. Where the latter is naturally poor, a self-pruning, which thins the bestand, begins earlier.

Rotation period.—In the northerly parts of the country two hundred, and on poorer ground three hundred, years are requisite for the pine to grow to good timber. In the southerly tracts one hundred years are sufficient. Free or open growing pine produces seed at fifteen to twenty years of age. But in close bestand it does not bear seed till the age of fifty to seventy years, after which every fourth year, on an average, can be reckoned on for seed. As the pine cones require about eighteen months to ripen, and the seed does not fall sooner than five to six months afterward, there is, therefore, discerned a coming seed-year already half another year before, by the yet small half-year-old cones.

Felling, with seed-trees.—Where the ground is favorable for the reception of seed, six to seven older, healthy-seed-bearing trees should be left to each quarter of an acre. Where the ground is covered with grass, or slopes to the south, or is unusually bare, seed-trees should be left so that the cones shall not be more than about sixteen feet from each other.

Seed.—The seed of the pine is in closed cones, ripens in the latter part of October, the year next after blooming, and can be gathered from the beginning of November to the beginning of April. As has before been stated, cones of three different ages are often found on the same tree, namely, those that have opened and discharged the seed, those that are two years old, and those that are one year old. The proper ones can be distinguished from the rest without difficulty. They have a conic form, brownish-gray color, close-shutting shell. are from one to one and a half inch in length, and are fixed near the base of the last year's cones. The one-year-old cones have their place at the end of the bud or twig, are round and of greenish color. Empty cones have extended shell, and are of a grayish-brown color. When gathered, cones should be preserved in a place free from dampness. If desired they may be kept unshelled a year, but should be protected from the sun and from air-currents. To facilitate opening of the burrs a certain degree of warmth is required, the best being from the sun. Degree of warmth 42° to 43° Celsius, sometimes 50°. Cones collected late in the winter do not require more than eight to twelve hours warmth of such degree as first mentioned; earlier ones a day. * * * When the seeds leave the cone they have film-like oblong wings, one end of which incloses the seed. * * * A pine cone contains twenty to thirty seeds. * * In purchasing them one must see that the weight has not been increased by being made damp for that purpose, as such treatment injures them; also that they have not been warmed in an oven, the heat in such cases often being too great. Seven hundred good seeds make an ort, Swedish weight, (a little less than a hundredth part of a pound.) A kanna of clean wingless seeds weighs 2.8 skalpunds.

9. The blending of trees.

The bestand of pine and spruce is incomparably the most important for Swedish forests. The spruce, which, at a higher age, affords sufficient shade for the ground and thereby maintains its fertility, compensates for what in this respect is lacking in the clean pine bestand, while the pine, on its part, "kernel full" or vigorous stems, supplies that want of exterior hardihood which is observable in the exclusively spruce bestand.

The bestand of fir trees, especially pine and spruce, with the birch, is a blending which is not difficult to effect, and merits much attention, especially as the birch in such society acquires finer form of stem and larger size than when it grows alone. * * * But as the birch does not preserve the fertility of the ground, it should not be the prevailing sort.

The bestand of fir and beech occurs in the southern part of the kingdom, with the beech sometimes the prevailing sort.

10. Bestand of beech and oak.

This blending, especially for the oak, is of the greatest importance, because no sort of tree contributes so powerfully as the beech to maintain the soil at the degree of fertility which is requisite for the oak. This blending occurs in the south part of the country, where the climate is adapted to the beech; but in that part north of where the beech flourishes the blending of the oak with fir trees is practiced, particular regard being paid to the selection of proper spots for the oak. * * With the beech the oak shows a growth not to be seen under other circumstances.

The above, though perhaps imperfect, translations from Mr. Björkman's treatise will tend to show something of its practical character.

VIII.—INSTRUCTION IN FORESTRY.—(See ante, sec. III, § 3.)

The principal institution in Sweden for instruction in forestry is the Royal Forest Institute, at Stockholm. It is pleasantly situated on a rise of ground in a grove close to the bridge as one turns from the city to enter the Deer Park. The course of study occupies two years, and the first term begins in June. Tuition is free. Candidates for admission must have sound health, be neither under eighteen nor over twenty-eight years of age, and must have passed an examination such as admits to the university, which includes a knowledge of the German language, and either the English or French. Among the studies pursued are the classification and division of forest, forest culture, and the quality of timber, forest technology, climate and soil, forest botany, forest insects, art of hunting, mathematics, forest and game laws, map-drawing, &c. Four pupils receive from the State a stipend, as assistance, of 250 rix-dollars each, per year. Graduates are regarded as members of the forest "stat" or establishment, and are in the line of promotion therein; their first appointment being that of assistant forester, which is generally received immediately after graduation and opens the way to their earning about 600 rix-dollars a year in surveying and other work connected with forest. In ten years they can be promoted to "Jäg mästere," or forester. Above this last office is the position of forest inspector which has been created for three or four years. 15,300 rix-dollars are annually appropriated for the support of the institute. There are four active instructors, namely, the director and three "lektors," or teachers.

Forest schools.—Besides the institute there are, in Sweden, six forest schools which are principally supported by the government and located at the following places: Tierps, Upsala County; Ombergs, Östergötland County; Böda, Calmar County; Daniels Lands, Christianstad County; Hunneberg, Elfsborg County; and Silbre, Wester Norrland County. Tuition at the forest schools is free, and besides ten pupils at each school receive board and lodging free. The course of study lasts eight months. Some knowledge of the common branches taught in the folk-schools is all that is required for admittance. A graduate of a forest school can be employed as a forest watchman at about 300 rix-dollars per year and use of a dwelling and patch of ground. The studies are mentioned in the accompanying translation of regulations in regard to the forest schools. The government offers to help support additional schools where local authorities take the initiatory steps to establish them. From the report of 1867, it appears that 21,850 pupils in the "folk" or common schools received instruction in horticulture and tree-planting. Among the prominent schools of forestry in Europe 's one at Tharrand, in Saxony, one at Neustadt-Eberswalde, in Prussia, one at Aschaffenberg, in Bavaria, one at Nancy, in France, and one at Mariaborum, near Vienna.

In Sweden it is the practice in every branch of the public service and department of instruction to allow money for the traveling expenses of persons sent abroad to obtain information ; and sums varying from 500 rix-dollars to 1,200 rix-dollars are often granted for traveling in foreign countries on forest purposes.

IX.—FOREST LITERATURE.

Having in another part of this report mentioned some of the Swedish authors on forestry, I will now refer to some other works and documents which merit the attention of people who are interested in forest culture in the United States.

A short but practical article on the *culture and management of forest trees*, by J. J. Thomas, is published in the annual report of the Department of Agriculture for 1864.

An article entitled *American Forests ; their destruction and preservation*, by F. Starr, jr., may be found in the annual report of the Department of Agriculture for 1865.

The report of the Department of Agriculture for 1870 also contains an interesting paper on the subject of forests.

Field, Forest and Garden Botany, by Professor Gray, of Harvard University, is undoubtedly very useful as a hand-book, and for elementary instruction.

The North American Sylva, by F. Andrew Michaux, with notes by J. Jay Smith, 3 volumes, Philadelphia, Rice, Rutter & Co., 1865. The father of the author, a Frenchman, devoted ten years, from 1785 to 1796, to a thorough exploration of the territory of the United States, accompanied by his son. The latter revisited the country in 1801, and again in 1807, making extensive researches, the result of which was published in Paris 1810–1813, with rich copper-plate engravings. The work was translated into English by Hillhouse, and printed in that language at Paris, 1819. The second English edition was brought out at New Harmony, Indiana, partly through the efforts of William McClure. The present edition of 1865, in three large octavo volumes, contains the original illustrations beautifully colored, and deserves a place in every public library.

The North American Sylva, or a description of the forest trees of the United States, Canada and Nova Scotia, not published in the work of F. Andrew Michaux, illustrated by 121 colored plates, by Thomas Nuttall, three volumes in two. Philadelphia ; Rice & Hart, 1857. The author of this work visited the United States in 1823, and remained several years making explorations. A standard authority.

The Trees and Shrubs of Britain, by J. C. Loudon, in eight volumes, second edition, London, Henry G. Bohn, 1854. In this work native and foreign trees are pictorially and botanically delineated and scientifically and popularly described, with their propagation, culture, management and uses in the arts, in useful and ornamental plantations, and in landscape gardening. The introductory chapters contain a historical and geographical outline of the trees and shrubs of temperate climates throughout the world. The first four volumes contain the text, with above 2,500 engravings. The other four volumes are devoted to portraits of trees on octavo and quarto plates. The work contains a mine of information in regard to trees, very much of which would be highly entertaining to the general reader. It was first published in 1838, and the author cites upward of two thousand works referred to therein, which shows the voluminous character of forest literature even then. I venture to quote here a brief passage from his introductory chapter on the *Inducements for tree planting :*

"Many persons, when recommended to plant, reply: 'Of what use is it to plant at my age ?' I can never hope to live to see my plants become trees.' This sort of answer does not, at first sight, appear surprising, if we suppose it to come from a person of sixty or seventy years of age, but we often hear it even from men of thirty or forty. In either case, such an answer is the result of error, founded on mistaken and prejudiced notions. We shall prove its incorrectness by matters of fact. In the year 1830 there were many sorts of trees in the arboretum of Messrs. Loddiges, which had been planted exactly ten years, and each of which exceeded 30 feet in height. Most of these trees have since been cut down for want of room, but we have the names and the measurement of the whole of them. There are, also, at the present time (December, 1834) many trees in the arboretum of the London Horticultural Society's garden, at Chiswick, which have been only ten years planted, and which are between 30 feet and 40 feet in height. Why, then, should any one, even of seventy years of age, assign as a reason for declining planting that he cannot hope to live to see his plants become trees ? A tree 30 feet high, practically speaking, will effect all the general purposes for which trees are planted ; it will afford shelter and shade, display individual beauty and character, and confer expression on landscape scenery." (Introduction, p. 9.)

The Forester, or a practical treatise on the planting, rearing, and general management of forest trees. By James Brown, wood-surveyor, and nursery-man. Stirling ; fourth edition, enlarged and improved. William Blackwood & Sons. Edinburgh and London : 1871. Large octavo ; pages 835. Undoubtedly the best work on the subject in the English language.

This author states that, within the last twenty years, he has sent out a very large number of foresters to situations, at salaries varying from $350 to $800 per year. He laments that there is not a school in Great Britain, where young men can learn efficiently all the branches of study in connection with forestry, and gives the following advice as to the way in which a self-supporting institution for the purpose may be established : " Let an arboricultural association be formed of some of the leading landed proprietors in the country, with a few men of science among them, having for their object the cultivation of trees on the most approved and improved principles of the age, and the training up of young men as foresters according to these principles, in order to fill the places of the existing foresters of the old school, and thus as early as possible bring about an improved state of arboriculture for the general welfare of the country.

" Then, supposing that such an association were formed, where and how is the field of their operations to be had ? Of course they could not undertake anything in a definite and practical way in respect to forestry without this. Such a field may easily be had, as there are many landed proprietors in this country who have more estates than one, and who would be willing. I have no doubt, to give over the woodlands on one of them for the purpose of forming an arboricultural school of it, of course under safe and proper conditions to both parties. The outline of the conditions might be made somewhat as follows: The proprietor, R. F., lets to the association —— ——, for a period of, say forty years from date, all the woodlands at present on the estate of A., extending to about 2,000 acres, as per plan of the property to be referred to, at an annual rent of £——. The several crops embraced to be thinned, and otherwise dealt with for their improvement in health and value by the said association, and according to a mode to be proposed by them and approved of by the said R. F., the proprietor, who is to sell the timber and other produce for his own behoof, the association to be paid by him for the labor performed by them in dealing with the works of thinning and otherwise improving the crops, as may be agreed upon all at the usual rates for such works : these to be agreed on between the association and the said proprietor's agent at the beginning of each year, and before the works commence for the season. And the said R. F., the proprietor, lets also to the said association, for the said period of forty years, for the purpose of being planted by them from time to time with suitable kinds of trees, as may be agreed on between the parties, that piece of waste land known as ——, and extending to 1,800 acres, at the annual rent of £——. This portion of land is let to the association on the understanding that, at the end of their lease the said R. F., the proprietor, shall take over all the crops that shall then be found growing on it, at a valuation to be settled by two neutral men of skill, mutually chosen, when the said R. F., or his heirs, will pay the association the full value that may then be made in respect to the crops of trees that may have been planted by them on said land. And it is to be understood that during the currency of the lease the said association shall have full power to manage the woods they may plant on said waste land in their own way and as they may think fit, and to use for their own behoof all proceeds arising from them ; it being understood, however, that all the crops they may plant shall be properly treated and trained, so as to insure their being valuable to the estate as a crop on the land, when they are handed over to the proprietor of the land at the end of the lease. And it is also agreed that the said association shall have no power to clear any portion of said crops of trees they may plant, nor any portion of any crops whatever, without the consent of the proprietor of the land.

" A president and vice-presidents, with directors, would have to be appointed, as also a secretary, a treasurer, and auditor. Next, the working-resident staff might be a manager, who would be accountable to the president and directors for the proper working of the objects of the association. He would be assisted by a professor of botany and vegetable physiology, and one of geology and chemistry, the latter combining physical geography and climatic science ; while he, the manager, would also have the assistance of a first-class practical forester, whose duties would be to carry out all the practical operations, under the directions of the manager, in dealing with the woods, and at the same time instruct and guide the pupils while at their various works in the woods.

" To accommodate a staff of this kind, together with, say fifty or sixty pupils, a convenient house would require to be provided, and as to whether the pupils would be resident in it or not, would of course depend on a careful consideration of all the circumstances in connection with the locality in which the field was situated. At all events, one-half of the pupils would require to attend at a given hour every morning, to hear lectures and other instructions on the subjects to be taught by the professors, while the other half would go out to work in the woods. These would return in the afternoon to get their course of instructions, while those who were studying in the morning would go out and take their places in the woods ; and in this way the routine of daily theoretical and practical instructions would be carried on. Of course a portion of the waste land would be taken up for planting every year, in order to have the young men trained to the proper way of doing it, as also thinning in the different plantations, with bark-stripping, pruning, where necessary, draining, &c. In short, all these branches of work would be undertaken every year on some portion of the crops; and as all the works would be performed by the pupils themselves, under the direction of the forester, every one would have the full opportunity of gaining practical experience, as well as theoretical knowledge, on the various branches of forestry. And it would be necessary to keep all the woods under the management of the association in the very best possible condition, so that their character might become a model for all others to imitate. And, besides, it would be desirable for the manager and his professors to visit, from time to time, the woods on other properties, and take with them their pupils to see them, when they would have an opportunity of comparing the management of other woods with that of those on their home district; and in this way the pupils would get much useful information and experience, within the shortest possible time, under the guidance of their teachers, and thus render them more intelligent and experienced than they would be were their observations confined to the woods on the home field alone.

"In dealing with the pupils, the amount of fees they would pay would, of course, depend upon whether they were lodged in the institution or not, and had bed and board provided for them. I should say that they should be resident in the institution, and all receive like treatment as to education, board, and lodging. If they were not resident lodgers, irregularity would be certain to ensue, and want of proper rule. Then, if lodged, £50 a year might be a fair charge for each pupil. At all events, it should not exceed this sum. In accounting with the pupils, they ought to have put to their credit and deducted from their fees at the end of each term, when settlement is made, the value of the work they perform in the woods, at a fixed rate per hour or per day, as may be arranged. This would make them more industrious than they otherwise would be, and make them take good interest in the works they were engaged in. This value of work would, of course, be refunded to the association by their account against the proprietor of the woods for the work performed in them by their pupils.

"In order that the pupils might be properly instructed in all the branches bearing on arboriculture, and to secure the professors and all concerned doing their duties, an examination of the progress made by the pupils should be made by the president and directors at the end of every six months, and awards put to the credit of the most proficient and deserving.

"As the young men become proficient in all the branches, (after three years' residence at the institution,) theoretical and practical, of forestry, and leave the institution, they should have each his certificate or diploma, stating his general acquirements and abilities, and whether he is *first, second,* or *third* class in his profession. These certificates should, of course, be given by the president and directors, and signed also by the professors; and they should form a guarantee to landed proprietors who might be in want of foresters that the holders are men of undoubted professional abilities, and worthy of being trusted with the management of their woods." (Pp. 43-47.)

The following are some of the recent standard German publications·

Säen und Pflanzen. Ein Beitrag zur Holzerziehung. Von Forstdirector H. Barckhardt. Dritte Auflage, Hannover, 1867.

Das Forst Kulturwesen nach. Theorie und Erfahrung. Von Joh. Phil. Ernst Ludwig Jäger. Zweite Auflage, Marburg, 1865.

Der Waldbau oder die Forst Productenzucht. Von Dr. Carl Heyer. Zweite Auflage. Leipzig, 1864.

Der Wald Seine Verjüngung, Pplege und Benutzung Von E. Landos. Zürich, 1-66.

Besides the works in Swedish already mentioned, are the following:

Handledning vid Skogars Indlening till ordnard hushållning, &c., of J. A. of Zellén, (with colored map.) Stockholm, 1860.

Vägledning i Skogshus hållning med en karta of Isr Ström, Upsala.

Handledning för Skogs hushallare i Finland of C. W. Gyldén. Helsingfors, 1857.

X.—LIST OF SOME OF THE MORE RAPID-GROWING TREES.

What is given under this head is compiled principally from the works of Michaux, London, and Brown.

Black Italian poplar (Populus acladesca.)—Grown on strong loamy soil, and sheltered situation, will in twelve years attain a height of 40 feet, with diameter of stem of nearly a foot. In England it has of late years been substituted for the cottonwood.

Ontario poplar (Populus macrophylla.)—Worthy of cultivation as a timber tree, especially on the sides of streams with a shallow soil; easily distinguished by its large heart-shaped leaves, some of which measure 10 inches from base to apex, and gummy and, in the spring, balsamic smelling buds. It has been found to attain the height of 50 feet in fourteen years. Said to be a native of New Hampshire. Easily propagated by cuttings.

The *cottonwood* (Canadian poplar) has in Europe attained the height of 50 feet ten years after planted, and is considered the best of all poplars for planting when the production of timber for profit is the object.

The *Lombardy poplar* is easily distinguished by its tall, narrow form ; thrives on tolerably good soil, and attains largest size in proximity to water. A tree near Brussels is mentioned which in fifteen years attained the height of 80 feet, with a trunk from 7 to 8 feet in circumference.

The *sycamore* (called also plane and buttonwood) flourishes best in a deep, loose, rich soil, in a cool, moist situation. When placed near water its growth is so rapid that in ten years it will attain the height of 40 feet, and in twenty years 80 feet, with a trunk 8 feet in circumference at three feet from the ground.

The *elm* grows rapidly in almost any soil or situation. Instances are given of trees attaining the height of 50 feet after fourteen years planted.

The *willow* (*Salix alba*) will grow to the height of 60 feet to 80 feet in twenty years, and thrives in dry uplands. This is also the most rapid-growing native tree of Sweden.

The *sugar-maple*, in rich, strong, sandy loam, has attained the height of 24 feet six years after being planted.

The *locust* requires a sandy loam, rich rather than poor, and a situation at once airy and sheltered. It is objectionable for hedge-rows or as scattered groups on arable land, on account of its roots extending close under the surface, and proving an impediment to the plow, and sending up suckers. It is a rapid-growing tree, and esteemed for fuel and timber. Plants in ten years from the seed attain a height of from 20 to 30 feet, or even 40 feet. Propagated with facility by cuttings of the roots, but the best mode is by seed.

The *European larch* is one of the most valuable species on account of its rapid progress and excellent timber. It requires a soil deep and porous, and is found in its perfection in its native localities, the Alps, on a soil formed from the natural decomposition of rocks. It should be reared from seed from its native localities. In England it attains the height of 20 to 25 feet in ten years from the seed. In the course of fifty years it will attain the height of 80 feet or upward. At ten years of age, on favorable soil and site, it is found to attain a diameter of 2 inches 8 feet from the ground ; in fifteen years a diameter of 5 inches ; in twenty years 9 inches ; in twenty-five years 11 inches. (On favorable soil and site in Scotland, at twenty years of age, and 8 feet from the ground, the oak attains a diameter of 4½ inches, the pine 6½ inches, the spruce 7 inches, the sycamore 5½ inches.)

The *Norway spruce* is the loftiest of European trees, attaining a height in some cases of 180 feet. On old trees the branches are gracefully drooping. Leaves are dark green. It grows most luxuriantly in deep loams and low, somewhat moist situations, or on acclivities with a northeast aspect and a moist, sandy soil. It is one of the best nurses for other trees. In ten years from the seed the plants will attain the height of 12 to 15 feet, and in fifty years the height of 90 to 100 feet. The wood is light, fine-grained, elastic, and varies in durability according to the soil on which it has grown.

C. C. ANDREWS.

LEGATION OF THE UNITED STATES,
        St. John, August 7, 1872.